PARADOX
and the
Christian Faith

TWO BOOKS

Hippie Convert

© 2016, 2019 James H. Kurt
All Rights Reserved.

Children of Light Publications 11/30/2019
ISBN: 978-1-7332154-5-9

First Published by AuthorHouse 09/07/2016
(ISBN: 978-1-5246-2643-3)

No part of this book may be reproduced, stored in a retrieval system, or transmitted by any means without the written permission of the author.

Nihil Obstat:
Rev. Msgr. Robert F. Coleman, J.C.D.
Censor Librorum
August 9, 2016

Imprimatur:
+ Most Reverend John J. Myers, J.C.D., D.D.
Archbishop of Newark, New Jersey
August 30, 2016

The **Nihil Obstat** and **Imprimatur** are official declarations that a book or pamphlet is free of doctrinal error. No implication is contained therein that those who have granted the **Nihil Obstat** and **Imprimatur** agree with the contents, opinions, or statements expressed.

TABLE OF CONTENTS

1. **PARADOX and the Christian Faith**......5
   - I 9
   - II 25
   - III 41
   - IV 56
   - V 72
   - VI 88
   - VII 104

2. **Hippie Convert**......119
   - I 123
   - II 163
   - III 191

Other Books by James Kurt......239

LORD, let my soul breathe with your peace and unity,
   my heart beat with your love and penitence,
   my mind shine with your wisdom and patience,
   my body be filled with your strength and humility,
   and my spirit reflect your innocence and truth.

1
PARADOX
and the
Christian Faith
(a spiritual guide)

Two Books

    May the LORD bless your spiritual life
    with His grace and wisdom.
    May you follow along His way,
    and so come into His presence.

Prologue

In the teachings of the Christ, as well as in His actions, there is paradox. The heart of this paradox, for Jesus, is found in His being God Himself, one with the Father, yet also a human being who has trod this earth; for us it is found in our being merely human, yet called to divinity in the heavenly Kingdom. With this distinction between Heaven and earth in mind, with our finger on the pulse of this paradox... all confusion should fall away, and we should understand the Word of God in the clear light of day.

> "The LORD is faithful in all His words
> and loving in all His deeds."
> Ps. 145:13

This always remember. However confusing things may seem, do not forget His love and truth.

Two Books

INTRODUCTION

The words of Christ can indeed seem confusing to the uninitiated mind, to him who thinks only as the world thinks, as selfish man has come to view life. For the world tells us to look out for number one and get all the money and power we can amass – this is the way to win the race. And so those who have not had a change of heart, those who have not put on the mind of Christ, how can they understand the teaching that "the last shall be first," or that "one must die to live"…? It will seem utterly confusing – *How can the last be first or death bring life? This Jesus is contradicting Himself!* Then when one manages to delve into what Christ means, and begins to comprehend what He intends to say – confusion readily turns to repulsion for the worldly soul: *He wants me to humble myself, to take the last place… to think of others more than myself…? He must be nuts!* And when the piece de resistance comes: "Love your enemy," the worldly soul balks: *Love my enemy!? I hate my enemy and all he stands for – I have no sympathy for that bum at all. I'm not gonna pray for him or give him my coat or turn the other cheek…. Now I know this Jesus really is nuts!* And so it goes. But what of those who recognize the wisdom (and love) in Christ's words? What of those who wish to immerse themselves as deeply as possible in His grace? This book is for souls such as these.

I

1. Abraham

Are you as Abraham? Are you seeking a new home, or do you wish to turn back to the world? You must set your face like flint and never turn back, if you would make progress. And progress is our goal here.

It must be stated first of all that the catalyst for growth in the spiritual life is suffering; it is this that engenders faith. Abraham, our father in the faith, may not have suffered physical tortures like Christ on the Cross or so many of our martyrs, but the essence of suffering he knew well. For though we may think primarily of pain when we consider suffering, at the heart of suffering is the call to wait.

This was the Lord's last word to His apostles, was it not: to wait, to watch, to be ready…? And if a thousand years are as a single day in the sight of God, how prepared we must be to wait! Three days Jesus endured His Passion, and they must have felt like three thousand years. And our father in the faith waited twenty years for the birth of his promised son, even as he approached one hundred years of age.

This is how the LORD works, very slowly, very gradually… and yet very quickly. After all, the Passion did last only three days; and was Abraham not called suddenly to leave his homeland with all his household in tow? And though he waited a while again, from Haran he was suddenly called to go forth once more. And to a place he knew not. Ahhh! Here is the truest sign of faith – to go as the LORD calls, without knowing how or where (or when). Then we know best His working in our lives, for then we are dependent on Him most. And is this not knowing, this needed trust, not greatly present in our having to wait on His will when it seems He does not hear us? (We wait for an eternity for our Lord to come, and in the end it is like the blink of an eye.)

2. The Cross

There is a book by an anonymous author (of the fourteenth century) titled *The Cloud of Unknowing*, which is perhaps the most profound spiritual guide. And perhaps St. John of the Cross, the Mystical Doctor, best explicates our need to enter this cloud of unknowing in order to draw closer to God. Indeed, we must sacrifice not only sensible pleasures and consolations but spiritual reassurances as well, taking no comfort in anything of this world if we are to find Him who transcends this world (yet loves it deeply). We must admit that we know nothing if the light of the LORD is to enter our minds.

Jesus tells us we must take up our cross daily and follow Him. He tells us, indeed, that we must lose our lives for His sake if we wish to find life everlasting. The world is shrouded in darkness, yet we are part of that world. How can we separate ourselves from the darkness of the world if we do not sacrifice our lives, if we do not take up our cross... if we do not lose attachment to this world of sin? And if we cling to this world and its sin (and our own place within it), how can we come to Jesus and find eternal life?

We cannot. The Cross is the way to eternal life. As surely as it is Good Friday that leads to Easter Sunday, so the path to Heaven is suffering, is the cloud of unknowing. We must

Paradox (I)

leave this world to find the new world. Nothing of this world can we allow to cling to us.

This does not mean that we neglect our duty toward work or family or church.... We continue in the world, but must not be *of* the world. We must use this world as if not using it; our hearts must be set on Heaven even as our feet tread this earth. For this world as we know it is passing away – and we must let it pass.

The LORD delights in those who wait for His love.

3. Mary

I do not wish to get too far into this work without mentioning the Blessed Virgin Mary, our Mother in the Faith. She is the true daughter of Abraham and the fulfillment of the faith that began with him. And she fully embraces the Cross with her Son.

As Abraham went forth without knowing where he was going, so did Our Lady in a most extraordinary way. From the first she walked by faith alone, unafraid of even the paradox of being called to marriage with Joseph after having vowed her virginity to the LORD. Her vow was most solemn and could not be broken, yet when led to marriage, she accepted, not knowing how this contradiction could be resolved: in the face of the impossibility of any resolution, she believed that God could do all things.

Does this not remind us of the predicament of Abraham, the impossible paradox he faced when the LORD called him to sacrifice Isaac, the promised son he had waited so long to hold in his arms? Yet he went forth with Isaac carrying the wood for the sacrifice and did not hesitate to tie him down, knife in hand. And YHWH intervened – at this moment with a ram and ultimately with His only begotten Son, whose Cross resolves all paradoxes of the Faith.

And so the LORD intervened miraculously to have the Virgin Mary conceive; and so Joseph, too, came to believe. And so she pondered all these things in her heart as her Son grew and made His way to the Cross. (Did she ever know what the next day would bring?) Though she hesitated in the temple when her Son was twelve and ready to begin His mission, when the time came she endured the Cross with Him in all its trial, in all its pain… and never did she waver in faith. Indeed, her heart was pierced and she suffered as He did, as completely as one can… though nails did not pass through her hands (these might have provided relief from her agony). Whose pain is greater, the one being crucified or the mother who must watch? She is only outdone by His being the Son of God.

4. Mother Teresa

In considering the Cross and the pain it brings – even the utter abandonment the Lord experienced thereon – one cannot help but think of Mother Teresa and the remarkable suffering she underwent being bereft of all consolation and finding herself immersed in darkness. Yet she brought more light to the world than any other soul of our time. Is there not great paradox in this contrast of dark and light, the deepest of doubt and the strongest of faith?

This is the paradox of all the saints, who recognize themselves as the worst of sinners, who even as they grow holier become more aware of just how far they are from the

Paradox (I)

presence of Almighty God. Those who consider not their place in relation to Him will know no darkness, will recognize no sin in their lives (and so receive no light); he who is pleased to live in a filthy house has no consciousness of the dirt surrounding him, and so no inclination to clean it. Only when one begins to clean the house does one see just how filthy his soul has become. And the closer we draw to God, the darker the world becomes.

Mother Teresa could find no consolation in the world; she became increasingly aware that everything of this world falls short of God's glory... yet her heart trusted in His presence and only His presence. She found His presence in the poor, of course, but not in a complete manner. She found it in the Sacrament and in adoration thereof... but still she desired the fullness of His Presence, not just to see through a glass darkly. And so darkness was upon her – and so she would find what she sought.

The closer she drew to Him, the more she confronted the darkness and doubt and went forward, the greater her faith became... till it became nearly complete, even on this earth. The Cross she carried in her bones, and so through her always light shone.

5. The Eyes of a Saint

It is true, the greatest joy is known upon the Cross... but also the greatest pain. One wonders why people were surprised to learn of the intense suffering Mother Teresa experienced for so many years. She always smiled – and insisted her sisters do the same – for without joy the call from the LORD is vain. But did no one look into her eyes?

Two Books

I once noticed this paradox of joy and pain in a photograph of St. Charles de Foucauld affixed to the door of my hermitage during a weeklong retreat. There he was, smiling broadly (and sincerely). Then I looked in his eyes and could see nothing but pain. I also witnessed this paradox in person in Vicka ("Vitska"), one of the alleged visionaries of Medjugorje. All the pilgrims remarked how beautiful her smile was, for indeed she was always smiling brightly. But when she paused a moment as she passed by me on her way to her porch to speak (smiling brightly as ever), looking in her eyes all I could see was pain.

You can see this pain in all the photographs of Vicka and Mother Teresa – it is unmistakable to anyone with eyes. And, again, it exemplifies the paradox of the saint, the paradox of the Cross: it reveals that (genuine) joy and pain are not separate or opposed but integrally bound together, especially on this earth.

The uninitiated soul thinks how wonderful it would be to be blessed as Mother Teresa with such closeness to the LORD – but she found this closeness amongst the most destitute on earth. Or how good it would be to have visions of Our Lady... but the visions last only for a time, and then one must return to the world. And how terrible the world can seem after having had this perspective of Heaven; and how intensely one then longs for heavenly fulfillment.

In every Joyful Mystery, Mary experienced pain: at the fearful appearance of the angel; in difficult travel; in giving birth; in a terrible prophecy; and in the apparent loss of her Son. And Jesus knew this pain better than any as He walked this soiled earth. He understood all and loved all and yet dealt day to day with those who continually misunderstood and lacked of love... all the while longing for the salvation of

Paradox (I)

our souls. On the Cross He accomplished that goal – and this brings the greatest joy to us all (and to Him who cares deeply for our souls). But only through indescribable pain was it done.

6. Pain and Joy, Continued

The Cross continues with us as it has with Mother Teresa and all the saints. We must be saints, too.

I don't know how well I can explicate this mix of joy and pain one finds upon the Cross and in general following the Lord. My own sacrifice falls far short of most others. But there have been times when I have had a profound sense of the Cross on my shoulders, weighing heavily upon my heart. This has mostly been in prayer.

I was once wont to pray the Sorrowful Mysteries every night before bed, taking nearly an hour to do so. Breathing in I kept my soul in silence (remembering God's NAME) and allowed the projection of an image of the mystery in my mind; breathing out I spoke a phrase of the prayers while raising my heart up to God (in sacrifice and praise). In this practice I can say I gleaned a distinct sense of the Cross.

There was joy in the pain of prayer and meditation on the sufferings of Christ, first because, indeed, I found myself sharing in Christ's pain – this is a joy in itself, for what greater blessing can we know than to be one with the Son of God even in His holy sacrifice? There was joy, too, because Christ's sacrifice brings salvation to man, and so my sharing in that sacrifice offered also a share in bringing His light to this world. And so I could rejoice inside that there was much good for others in my prayer.

But this mixture of pain and joy goes deeper still (though "mixture" is not really the right word, for they are not mixed as if they could later be separated out, but are fused as one, dependent upon one another for their existence). It is the suffering itself that causes joy, since suffering breeds love in our souls and it is the sharing in love – best demonstrated by Jesus' sacrifice on the Cross – that brings us joy.

Do you begin to see the interplay, the union of joy and pain, my brother, my sister? Remember God's love and it will not escape you.

7. Breeding Love

How does suffering breed love? It is the brokenhearted the LORD saves; the humble and contrite of heart receive His mercy – with the poor in spirit He shares His love.

When we have compassion for others, when we share their pain, weeping with those who weep, are not our hearts refreshed, do we not discover the depth and breadth of life? The worldly mind looks upon sitting at the bedside of the sick and dying as a waste of valuable time: he could be out making money or increasing his reputation. Every minute that passes another dollar ticks away…. He lives in a world of vanity.

But the enlightened mind finds in these moments what life is all about – he finds love… a beating heart, a breathing soul. He slows down and comes into the (silent) presence of God, leaving the world's illusions behind. And the one in the bed knows this better than he, if he is likewise illumined; if he has accepted the grace of his suffering, uniting it with Jesus' own, he is able to draw that much closer to God (even as the world fades into the background).

Paradox (I)

God is love. And God is not known to those who rush through their days intent on the things of this world, suffering only from selfishness and pride. This is vain suffering. This is pain with no glory of redemption. It is but death, not life. And so, would it not be a grace, or at least provide the means to grace, if that ignorant soul (who is like us all) were suddenly confronted with a crisis that halts the train on which he has been traveling in such emptiness? (And will we answer this call to faith?)

God wishes evil on no man. He would not see us suffer. But He loves us and turns all things to good if we but seek to share in His love. He is very patient and desires the salvation of all; and so, let us suffer with Him for all straying souls. And we shall know love.

8. The Humbled and the Exalted

Perhaps it is time to explore Jesus' central teaching, and central paradox: that the humbled are exalted (and the exalted humbled). Actually, we have touched upon it already in speaking of the sacrifice a Christian must make and the suffering he must undergo to find the love of God... but let us address it more directly.

The saint is indeed the soul who sees himself as a terrible sinner; and one can but be condemned if his pride becomes his greatest treasure. We must remain humble, always humble... ever more humble as we draw ever closer to God, for what are we in His sight but lowly creatures unable even to conceive of His glory?

Jesus was humble, the humblest of all. God is more humble than a speck of dust. It might amaze us – as it should

Two Books

– to think of God as infinitely humble, but Jesus has shown us that this is so. His love makes Him humble, causes Him to leave His Father's side to walk amongst us sinners. And He does not become humble only in becoming incarnate – He is humble in His very being. The Father and the Holy Spirit are thus humble as well. They think of us rather than themselves; and with Jesus they are ready to sacrifice all to save our souls.

God is humble, too, because He is Spirit: He is not of this earth at all. He is beyond it and above it and outside it… and nothing of it holds any sway over Him. Yet He cares intimately for all upon it, for it is His own Creation.

And we must become as He is – this is His desire. We must become as Spirit, one with the Spirit of God, leaving behind all of this world. And in this poverty, in this abandonment of all that is of the earth, is the great humility to which we are called, which will lead us to the Kingdom of God. Humility is our way to Him, but we should remember He has gone before us and desires our exaltation at His side. And so, be attached to nothing of this world.

9. St. Francis

Perhaps St. Francis lived this blessed humility better than anyone, except for the Blessed Mother. He is the quintessential saint, the image of Christ (as he has been called). Did he not famously wed himself to Lady Poverty? Did he not freely give up all his many possessions – for he was the son of a wealthy man – to find the grace of following in Jesus' steps most perfectly? Did he not hear best the Lord's call to sell all we own and give it to the poor that we might better follow Him?

Paradox (I)

And he did this while still dwelling in the world, walking among men. He did not go into the wilderness to be alone with God – which is certainly an admirable call as well, a holy and beautiful one indeed – but practiced his utter poverty while still interacting with others who were not so inclined. He did have brothers and sisters who joined him in his call, and this must have been a comfort and encouragement to him, but his poverty was accentuated by being with those who continued in the world. Much as Jesus did, he stayed among the people, which likely made remaining poor all the more difficult.

He knew well the poverty, the emptiness of self to which Christ calls all souls. And so he is much to be admired, and much to be imitated. One may question how well those who wear the habit today follow in his way, or how well any could, but he should be held up as an ideal, as one whose life it would be wise to embrace.

For then we would be blessed as he who even bore the wounds of our Lord in his very body. Then we would be blessed as he who cried his eyes to blindness. Then we would be raised from this soiled earth to walk the paths of Heaven.

10. Death

What is more paradoxical about the Christian Faith than death? YHWH is the God of Life – He is Life: I AM is His NAME and He breathes life into all creatures and desires life for all His Creation, and eternal life for man. Yet we find this life only by death.

The Cross is the ultimate sign of death. It symbolizes the worst death a man can undergo. Crucifixion is the culmination of man's devising of death, the culmination of the worst that is in him. Yet Jesus died on the Cross, and without His death we would still be dead in our sins.

This is the key to understanding the paradox: discovering the difference between being dead in sin – and thus dead in soul – and being dead in body... the physical death we all must endure. They may go together but are not the same. And for the Christian, the former is by far the worse.

God never intended death, never wished it for His creatures... but we have brought it about by our sin (and so spiritual death leads to physical death). Yet He takes what our hands have wrought and makes it into a blessing for our souls. For He is never outdone. Death is now a remedy for our misery, for the death we know by our sins.

If we were to continue in our sin, if our hands were to reach out to the Tree of Life in our corrupted state – what hell we would know forever! But as it is, death, and specifically the death of the Son, saves us from such a fate. Not only is there a merciful end to our mortal misery, but separation from God is itself overcome. And so we are called to die to sin and be ready to leave this life that we might live again with the LORD. This is the death that is a blessing: dying to a life of sin.

11. Self-Emptying

Let us look more closely at how this blessed death is at work in the Christian soul. We may understand it better by considering self-emptying, which is itself a kind of death.

Paradox (1)

We are told that Jesus emptied Himself to come among us, and while among us He emptied Himself of all He had taken on. And this self-emptying we must imitate.

We must empty ourselves of all attachments to the things of this world, certainly; if not going as far as Francis in selling everything and giving it to the poor, at least by not holding on to what we don't need and being ready to give all away if necessary. But internally as well we must be emptied, most notably of our pride.

What an obstacle is pride and self-will to the spiritual life! Nothing is more dangerous to us than being attached to ourselves, to our gifts and talents (real or imagined) and putting our trust in them rather than the LORD. We are nothing without God – this must never be forgotten, lest we die.

It is a constant struggle not to be filled with ourselves, not to become complacent and self-satisfied and so begin to think we do not need God... and eventually to forget Him all together. This is the real death. This is true vanity, the sign of a worthless life. From this may the LORD save us!

Let us rather continually empty ourselves of ourselves and any thought for ourselves that we may never be tempted to such vanity. We must check ourselves every day to see if we are dying to our pride and living for God. To our bowels we should sense this self-emptying, as we surrender our very body and blood to the LORD and allow ourselves to be filled with His presence alone.

Then we begin to live, when we lay down our arms so thoroughly that we find we have nothing in us but Him. Then we join our Savior on the Cross, emitting a groan of helplessness as we offer all we are into the Father's hands. (Then He will not hesitate to take us in His arms.)

12. Silence

The silence of the LORD is thunderous, though gentle. It fills the universe yet is perfectly still. The tongue cannot speak of God, cannot name Him, for He is beyond words even as He is beyond space and time. Yet He is very present.

His NAME itself is Silence (YHWH). It silences the tongue that speaks it. The whole universe is silent before our Almighty God, and we must be silent, too, showing due reverence to the LORD.

How shall we find this silence within ourselves? Yes, by emptying ourselves of all that is of the world.... This is necessary. But the key is in the tongue. As the tongue has the power to set the whole body, the whole universe aflame, so when it is stilled, everything else follows along. And so the LORD has given us His NAME.

Speak His NAME – "YHWH" – and His Silence will be upon you; while His Silence is upon you, you will be speaking His NAME. For it is Silence. For it silences the tongue. O what divine paradox is here in the NAME of God! Could anything compare with such wonder, such beauty, such Truth? His NAME is *pronounceable silence*. This silent WORD speaks volumes; indeed, it fills the universe... and yet it may be upon our tongues. What a gift! Pronounce this silent WORD and your tongue will be stilled, and you will enter into His Silence.

On the Cross (and now in the Sacrament upon our altars) the Divine Silence has spoken most clearly, most poignantly. All that Jesus had, all that He was, He gave to the Father... and what was left but silence? But His death is not the last word; this silence He speaks upon the Cross is not the mere absence of sound – it is God's thunderous voice filling the universe, gently, and completely. Listen for that voice, my brother, my sister, and let it fill you.

13. Meekness

Scripture tells us Moses was the meekest man on the face of the earth, this servant who was the LORD's great prophet, who spoke to Him face to face – with whom the LORD shared His NAME. His meekness was like Jesus' own.

None is more gentle and lowly than Jesus. Moses was a blessed reflection of Him, but none could compare with God Himself. And Jesus calls us to be the same.

Meek and humble of heart. It is not how the world judges greatness; it is not the vision the world has of the Almighty God. Yet this is what He is, He Who Is the greatest amongst us, He Who holds the world in His hand.

Quietly the LORD comes to us, not shouting, not boasting of His glory. Of His glory there is much to boast... but He is therefore more humble and gentle with us. He wishes to draw us into His loving heart.

On Mount Horeb the LORD revealed Himself to Elijah in a still, small voice. Not in the earthquake, or in the fire – He is not known in the power of mighty horses or in warriors' strength, but in a quiet heart, in a humble soul. What more does He ask of us than to tremble before Him and do His will.

This Elijah did. This Moses did. This Jesus did in the most perfect way. This we are called to do: be humble, be gentle, be quiet... find His Spirit working through us by the power from on high. (O LORD, let me be the meekest man on the face of the earth!)

14. The Still Point

T. S. Eliot uses a beautiful turn of phrase in his poetry, "The still point of the turning world," to refer to the transcendent center of all Creation, where God rests, where the LORD dwells among us. And we must be still before Him to find it, to keep ourselves from being distracted by all the chaos around us.

Like the hub of a wheel is this still point: the world moves around it and depends upon it for its movement, but it does not move. The world goes round and round, separating itself from God, from its center, and the vanity grows each day as this becomes a darker place... but God does not move, does not change – He remains with us always at the heart of existence, and we must keep Him present in our own hearts, lest we spin out of place with the world in its rebelliousness.

We can turn; we can move, yes. There is nothing evil in this... but we must keep the LORD at our center. If He is indeed in our hearts, our movements will be blessed and we will be doing His work in this world; but, again, if we become separated from Him, our lives become vain.

How wonderful is the still point! How marvelous to find it present in our souls, breathing in us even with the Breath of God. Then we are blessed to be sons and daughters of a loving Father and brothers and sisters to the Lord Jesus. Then we have the Spirit upon us.

The Spirit moves among us; like fire it burns throughout Creation. Let it be this holy fire that is with us and not the fires of this world (or of hell). We must remove ourselves from all unholy fire and find the LORD of all speaking in our hearts and moving in our lives. (Make your home at the still point.)

II

1. The Last Shall Be First

There is not much difference between saying "the humbled are exalted" and "the last shall be first." Both are equally paradoxical, both capture the essence of Christ's teaching, and both call us to be lowly. But perhaps this taking of the lowest place (in order to follow Christ) is made somewhat clearer by the word "last," particularly in our very competitive society.

To be the last seems a more specific call, and so a more difficult one, than simply to be humble. Humility may have a number of connotations, some more appropriate than others, and so some of the most appropriate ones may be conveniently overlooked by a soul wishing to rationalize away the severity of Christ's call. But to be the last, the least... here there are fewer loopholes.

We have said that the saints (to a man, or woman) see themselves as the worst of sinners. If this striving for holiness were indeed a race, they would be convinced of their coming in last place. Of course, they are not – you can see that and I can see that (and the Church can see that)... but they see what they see; and they see themselves falling thoroughly short of accomplishing the LORD's will. (We, too, would see there is so much more we could do, so much better we could be, if we looked at ourselves through God's eyes.)

And taking the last place in daily life, where the rubber meets the road – how much harder this is than thinking of things abstractly. We are so inclined to see ourselves as better than others and able to do things better than they... how hard it is to say, "You are more deserving" (and this to every person!). But this is what we must do. We must be ready to say (and mean) that others deserve to enter the Kingdom before we do, and hold the door open for them, knowing that if we are patient, the LORD will call us, too, when everyone else is in. And then the celebration will begin.

2. The LORD Chastises Those He Loves

Thus love and chastisement are equated in the LORD, chastisement being a sign of His love. If we are not chastened by Him, we do not know His love.

The message of repentance is for us all, and is Christ's essential call. And this message shows that He loves every soul. There is no one whom the LORD does not chastise, for He loves us all and would thus draw us into His heart, away from the dangers of a sinful world. But who hears His call? Who treasures His chastisement? It is these who answer love with love and are embraced by the Father.

No one escaped Jesus' chastisement: He chastised the Pharisees and the leaders of the people; He chastised the people themselves for their dullness of heart; He chastised His apostles, even calling their leader a "Satan"; and He chastened even those whom He healed from sickness and saved from death – telling the adulterous woman and the man at the pool of Bethesda to "sin no more," lest a worse fate befall them.

The LORD chastises every soul, reveals to our eyes the sin dwelling within us – the question always is: what is our reaction? Do we welcome such blessing and admit our sin before Him, crying out for His forgiveness and healing (which He is always ready to give); or do we harden our hearts like

Paradox (II)

Pharaoh, inviting greater chastisement, as the LORD continues to seek our souls?

If we turn away, He cannot turn away: He remains always faithful to His love for us. And the harder our hearts become, the more pain of separation we experience.... O how He would keep us from wailing and grinding our teeth in outer darkness! But our hearts must soften to His call. O LORD, save us from our foolish pride!

3. Turn

A term that is often used along with the call to repentance is "turn." We are called to turn from our evil ways and walk the way of the LORD.

The word "turn" is used because it gets across the change that must be made – a 180° turn is required, for the ways of the world are diametrically opposed to those of God. It does not refer to a physical turning (though we may indeed literally notice our feet traveling in the wrong direction at times) but is meant to convey more so a turn of the mind and heart to God, a metanoia, if you will.

And this change that is required of us is constant; we do not turn once and then that is it. There may be very dramatic moments in our lives when the turn to the LORD is more extreme – as was Paul's on the road to Damascus (and certainly the most dramatic turn for each of us is made at our Baptism); still, every day we must give our hearts to God, for every day the world presents itself before our eyes with the call to walk in its ways.... And so every day and at all times we must be on guard, recognizing our need always to change our ways, continually to turn away from the world to the LORD and His love.

Repentance is a daily practice for the committed Christian. Turn to Him, my brother, my sister. Do not be afraid and do not hesitate. He waits for you; He longs to see your face. And when you walk toward Him, it is His face you will see... and its light will lead you forth. Walking away from Him, turning your back to your Creator, what will you find but darkness, growing darkness with every step you take? Stop in your tracks this day and turn to face His glory. (Ever more turn your heart and mind to Him.)

4. Baptism

I have been writing with the presumption that my reader is a baptized Christian (probably a Catholic), but since this writing may come into the hands of someone not yet baptized, I ought to say a word about this most important of sacraments.

First let me say, if you are indeed not yet baptized, do not wait, do not linger in any hesitation. If you have questions, ask them; if bothered by doubts, pursue clarification. You may find some answers here but you cannot have a conversation with a book – seek out a good priest or other faithful Christian to respond to your particular concerns. But do not waste time. The clock is ticking and Jesus awaits.

This sacrament is a necessity. You need to be cleansed of original sin and given grace to combat the devil. It is possible without Baptism you could still be saved (with the LORD all things are certainly possible), but do not shun this ordinary means and presume upon the LORD's grace and patience. It

Paradox (II)

is not wise, and will not help. Embrace the means He has given, the sacrament He has instituted, and join with your brothers and sisters in Mother Church. Beware the sin of pride.

And those who may be baptized but not Catholic, and, indeed, those who may be Catholic and still question the Church's teachings – I say the same to you: Ask your questions, honestly, with a heart sincerely seeking truth. Allow your Mother to explain Herself before you walk away – beware the sin of pride.

Mary is the Saint of saints, "full of grace," as even the Angel of God declares; and by her own mouth the Spirit proclaims that "all generations will call [her] blessed." And would you hesitate to do so? Beware the sin of pride. The Eucharist is Christ's Body and Blood – He means what He says. If your faith falls short, beg His light, ask Him to show Himself to you.... Do not remain in fear and doubt.

And those who are baptized and find themselves faithful: You are blessed to believe all that the Church teaches, but beware judgment of others – for the soul who is not yet baptized or who doubts the Church's teachings may yet overcome you in the race to Christ. Beware the sin of pride.

5. His Burden Is Light

Yet another paradox of Jesus' teaching, of His Way. For it cannot but be said that His burden, which is the Cross we are all encouraged to carry, is heavy, very heavy.... One cannot even conceive of the weight Jesus bore in carrying the sins of the whole world. And as I say (as He says), we are called to join Him there.

Two Books

How can this heaviest of burdens be light? What do we find when we shoulder it with Christ? First we find it is He who bears the brunt of the burden. He does not leave us to carry even the (enormous) weight of our own sin alone but yokes us to Him that He might make our burden light. In fact, we find when we take up our cross with Him that it is indeed then things become lighter... for the Cross itself buoys us up with Jesus' grace.

This burden seems very heavy when we look at it from the outside, as we contemplate taking it up, for it requires our leaving our sins behind... and this can seem a terrible weight to bear. Here is indeed where the heaviness comes in, and so the lightness as well: when we cling to our sins, treasuring them above all things (especially our salvation), what a tremendous burden it seems to think of giving them up! The sins themselves are the burden, you see. And so when we do bring ourselves to give them up, to lay this burden down... what a marvelous lightness we find to the depths of our soul (one which touches even upon the body)! How many blessed souls have witnessed how the weight was lifted from them as they came from Confession, how they felt filled with light and walking on air...? Thus is His burden light, for He takes all burdens from us, and draws us into His loving heart.

6. St. Joseph

What if you were a humble and just man and found yourself betrothed to the Spouse of the Holy Spirit and Mother of the Son of God, essentially putting you in the place of the Heavenly Father? Would not any man who has a clear

Paradox (II)

sense of his lowliness run from such a situation, finding himself utterly unworthy and unprepared?

It is usually assumed that Joseph decided to divorce Mary quietly because of some kind of shame at having been cuckolded. But Joseph must have known Mary was a particularly blessed woman all along, and there is no reason for him to think her a liar or an adulteress. Scripture quotes the Angel as telling Joseph not to be "afraid" of taking Mary into his home, not that he needn't be ashamed. Joseph was experiencing a holy fear all of us would do well to learn, to find in our own souls.

Joseph was a particularly righteous man, a particularly holy man (second only in sainthood to Mary), and it is indeed this holiness and humility that made him realize how unworthy he was to be wed to the Mother of God and care for the only Son. A prouder person might not have blinked, might have thought the LORD's call appropriate to his status.... Thus it is only the lowly the LORD calls to do great things in His NAME.

Here is a caveat much to be understood and cherished, especially by those among us who receive a special call. And so it applies in a particular way to priests and religious... but every one of us is a child of God and called to do His will in this world, and so we must all be ever on our guard against assigning to ourselves what can only be accomplished by the LORD.

7. God's Will

God's will vs. man's will. Here is an essential distinction. When Joseph accepted the profound call to take Mary (and

Jesus) into his home, he was doing God's will, and accomplishing it by the power of God. Contrasted with him are those who go by their own power, who look only at themselves.

God calls the humblest, the meekest. Thus He called Moses, Joseph, Gideon (the least in his clan, which was of the least of the tribes), David (the youngest of his brothers and a mere shepherd boy), and of course the lowly virgin, Mary. He chose fishermen and a tax collector among His apostles. He calls the least to do the greatest because they know that they are nothing, that of themselves they can do nothing... because they have ultimate trust in God.

Those who do not do the will of God live in fear of God; this is true of men all the way back to Adam. This was true of Saul, who hid himself amongst the baggage when called to be presented as king. In this he was not being humble (as Adam was not in hiding from the LORD); his was not a holy fear like that of Joseph or David – whose heart was with the LORD and remained with the LORD (despite his sins) once the Spirit rushed upon him.... Saul's was a false humility, a lack of faith, a failure to trust in God (though He had given him, too, His Spirit).

It is the difference between Mary and Zechariah: Mary questioned not because she doubted God's ability to do as the Angel said, but because he seemed to be calling her to break her solemn vow of virginity. (Thus once she hears of Elizabeth's blessing – prayer for which, I propose, was the catalyst of her vow – she gives herself entirely to the LORD.) But Zechariah doubts God, looking only at himself – thus he is silenced. Joseph is a silent soul, but not from doubt or fear but out of humility and a genuine reverence for the LORD. His silence is the speaking of the NAME of God, whereas the silence of Zechariah is emptiness, a separation from the LORD.

Those who are truly humble and do God's will and not their own are blessed; those who are without faith and trust only in themselves are cursed. We must recognize the difference, in the Word of God and in ourselves.

8. St. Faustina

One of the most intriguing stories of St. Faustina regards an occasion when she was given a 'Glory Be' as penance following Confession. She went back to the priest some time later and asked for another penance because she was unable to complete the prayer. It is truly remarkable and indicates just how blessed a saint she was.

Can you begin to understand her situation, my reader? I have barely a crumb of the loaf from which such blessing comes, but it is enough to glean a sense of her predicament. One would have to realize, first of all, just how awesome, how overwhelmingly wonderful and fearful is our God... and so how astounding it is to call upon His Name.

We tend to take the LORD for granted. All of us. And so St. Faustina's story may seem almost funny to some, and mystifying to most. To understand it we must first realize how we indeed take God, and prayer to God, for granted... and seek diligently to overcome such complacency.

The truth is we should be speechless before the LORD, absolutely speechless (thus is His NAME, YHWH, divine Silence). Any word we say of Him is a distraction from and a reduction of His eternal glory. It is this Faustina felt and knew. She herself said that silence is the language of God.

Two Books

And how blessed she was to enter into that overwhelming silence.

Does this mean we should not pray? Only if the LORD takes all words from us, as He did on this occasion for Faustina. Otherwise, of course not. We are human beings and unless we are mute (or a hermit in the desert) we must use our voice. And though our words fall short of God's glory, the paradox is that they must be said; and that they bring us closer to the LORD if we pray with a sincere heart, with a mind that knows we fall short and a soul that desires to enter His silence. (His silence can be in every word.)

9. Words of Silence

Words, except of course for the NAME of God (YHWH) are made of sound – without sound they cannot be. The differing sounds constitute the different words. And so, how can words be of silence?

Words are sound, yes, but they are much more than this: they are of the Spirit, especially if they are words of truth inspired by the LORD. And so the words of the Gospels, the words of Holy Scripture, these words are more than sounds – they are the communication of the will of God to man by the power of the Holy Spirit. The Spirit is at the heart of the words.

And if the Spirit is at their heart, then silence, divine Silence, is the foundation on which they are set. They would be nothing without the Spirit but the sound of babble (or serve the spirit of the evil one); with the Spirit they are the most powerful force on earth. The sounds themselves thus become incidental, secondary to the Spirit that moves the tongue.

Paradox (II)

Here we confront the Logos, the Word, the Light and Logic of the LORD and His holy presence and will. In Scripture is contained the Divine Silence itself – these words express the Silence of God. His NAME speaks in them all.

And it is these words we must speak; the Truth we must always seek. It is not the Bible alone that expresses the Spirit of God (though only it does so in a perfect way): we are children of the LORD and must speak always His holy NAME in all we say... lest we speak in vain. Inevitably we fall short of such perfection, but it is this perfection, this perfect and all-encompassing Truth, to which we are called and which we can obtain by the grace of God. Let us always speak in silence, remembering the NAME of the LORD.

10. The Bronze Serpent

Look upon the bronze serpent (Jesus on the Cross) and live. See there your sins, what you have done to Him, and recognize, too, His love for you. He has been lifted up for your sake.

In the desert, at the LORD's command Moses made a bronze serpent and mounted it on a pole, that all who had been bitten by serpents for their disobedience might look upon it and live. And so they did. There they saw the mercy of God, and felt it to their bones.

How much more deeply the mercy of Christ sinks into those who are redeemed by His sacrifice, who look to Him for their salvation. It goes beyond being healed of a poisonous bite – it is the gateway to eternal life. And so I encourage all to look upon the Cross, and Jesus fixed there.

Two Books

God is nothing if not merciful, especially in His relationship with us humans. There is nothing we need more from the LORD than His infinite mercy. For we are sinners, every one; it is by our hands Jesus has been nailed to a tree... and how can we be forgiven this and escape the death we deserve except by the mercy of God?

He welcomes us with open arms. He is not ashamed to be murdered for our sake. Such is His love. Do you know His love bleeding there for you upon the Cross? Do not turn away from it or the recognition of your sin: it is all that can save you.

O LORD, may we all be saved by the sacrifice of your Son, a sacrifice that is scandal to half the world and absurdity to the rest. May all men's hearts open to the grace that pours forth from there, that Paradise might be ours again.

11. Satan's Defeat

I have noticed something in my spiritual life, particularly with regard to suffering, or evil of any kind (though perhaps one should seek confirmation of it in the lives of the saints and the teaching of the Church).

All evil comes from the evil one. Though the LORD allows it and though He makes it the means of our salvation (by the evil Jesus suffered at our hands and those of the devil), it is not in His will. He does not wish to see anyone suffer. And so, it is indeed the work of the devil. When we suffer it is at his hands.

But when we accept that suffering, when we even thank the LORD for the suffering that comes our way – and our prayer is sincere – it is then the devil removes the suffering from us, for he wishes not for us to find benefit in what he has wrought for our destruction.

Thus is he thoroughly frustrated by the free sacrifice of Christ on the Cross, who declares openly that it is the Father's will He accomplishes by the laying down of His life (and that He forgives us this sin). Here the turning of the tables on the devil is complete; here Satan is stripped of any power, even the power of evil – and we may join in that blessed fulfillment of the will of God, the utter defeat of the devil and his ways, by joining Jesus in praising the Father even for the suffering that is ours today.

Then the suffering will be gone. Then the evil one will have power no more. For if we make the darkness he attempts to sow in our lives into a source of great light... then darkness is no more. The devil is defeated.

12. The Will of God

The fool asks, "What does it matter what I do if God knows what I am going to do anyway?" He is not a fool for recognizing the omniscience of God – truly the LORD knows everything. He is a fool for arrogating to himself such knowledge, presuming to pronounce on what God knows when His thoughts are far above our own.

The wise man realizes he does not know the mind of God; and so he concerns himself with what he does know: the *will* of God, and his own will. God's will is only for our good. He desires every soul to enter into His presence, His Paradise... but each man has his own free will. Thus the wise man continually seeks to discern if his will is in accord with that of the LORD. Does he walk in His way?

How different this is from the thought of the fool, who seeks but to justify remaining in sin, turning from the call to repent by way of excuse. Laziness or lust or greed or pride or any of a number of sins has seized upon him, and he takes comfort therein, unwilling to relinquish its hold on him… and so he attempts to blame God for his condition.

But it will not work – this the fool knows in his heart – for God is only love. And though He takes all blame upon Himself (because of His love for us poor humans), if we fail to recognize His sacrifice, if we do not embrace His love and answer the call to walk with Him on right paths unto the Kingdom of Heaven, hardening our hearts against Him instead – where will we find ourselves but still in the devil's grasp, where we desire to be? And it will not matter what questions we ask.

13. What Is Above

God is What Is (YHWH, I AM), and certainly He is what is above. He is not what is below. Though He created the earth and all it holds and walked upon it as Man, He did not make sin nor participate in it at all… and it is sin (and death) to which we primarily refer when we speak of "what is below" – and God and His Kingdom when we say "what is above."

Are we of what is above or what is below? Are we of the LORD or of the evil one, who is the great sower of sin and death? Clearly, we are called by the Lord and His apostles to what is above, where He Is; but how well do we answer that call? And to what degree do we remain rooted to this world? This question we must answer day to day.

Paradox (II)

We are encouraged by Paul to clear out the old leaven, that of wickedness, of sin, and set our minds and hearts on what is above, finding the yeast that will cause us to grow unto Heaven. But is this our desire? Do we show it in our lives?

We know that so many have little interest in the things of God, setting all such talk aside to focus their attention on what is before their eyes, what appeals to their earthly desires. How immersed is the world in itself (drowning in sin as in Noah's day). And of its desperate state it seems almost unaware. And we who call ourselves Christians, are we aware of the surrounding dangers, and the fire that is coming upon the earth? Do we strive against this tide, or do we float downstream with the dead things?

O let us set our sights on what is above, where Jesus waits in eternal life!

14. Blessings in Disguise

The LORD's blessings often come in disguise. The most obvious of these is the death of God on the Cross. As has been said, there could be no greater horror, no greater curse, if you will... and yet this horror is the source of all blessings for mankind.

But wisdom must note that even in this, things are not so black and white; there is further paradox. One cannot simply say that the curse is now a blessing, for the curse remains a curse (just as a man's sins remain sins), even though the LORD uses it to turn the tables on all curses, on all sin, and indeed makes it our greatest blessing.

We must not get confused and think that somehow it is "good" that we sin, since it brings the grace of Christ's blood upon our souls. It is not *sin* that brings the blessing; to be clear, sin remains sin. *Repentance* of sin – the need of which itself illustrates the horror of sin – is what invites the LORD's blessing. And so, though where sin abounds grace abounds all the more, this is due to the abundant mercy of God *despite* our sin, not because of it.

And so in all blessings that come in disguise we must clearly discern the good from the evil and not conflate the two. The greatest blessing Mary knew was to become the Mother of God. This blessing, of course, came with a 'curse' – the piercing of her heart with Jesus' own – and it was also founded in a curse, if you will.

Mary had shown the self-sacrifice exemplified in Christ by offering her own virginity that (it is evident to me) Elizabeth might conceive. As Elizabeth's conception is a great grace, so Mary's giving up her fertility is, in itself, a kind of curse, something to be grieved. One cannot say, pointing to her sacrifice, that motherhood is thus not a blessing – using Mary's offering as an excuse for selfishness. Mary endured this 'curse' that a blessing might come to her kinswoman… and then received by the Angel the greatest blessing of all.

III

1. Baptized into His Death

Baptism brings new life, eternal life, to our souls. But first we must die.

As we are plunged into the waters of Baptism, as they pour upon us, we are joined to the glorious death of Jesus – we die with Him. And though He is the only one who actually dies, the only one whose blood is shed, He joins us to this sacrifice that we might know its fruits, that is, new life.

Here again we see the interplay of death and life that is so much a part of our Christian faith: death to sin and life to God, this is what the faith is all about. And so we should not concentrate too narrowly on either one, risking the exclusion of the other, for truly both are one and cannot be separated. And those who lose one or the other, lose both.

Death and new life come to us simultaneously in our Baptism; there is not a breath of space or time between them. As we die, so we rise. As we embrace Christ's holy sacrifice on the Cross, making it our own, standing in His stead... so new life, the glory that is inherent in the sacrifice, is ours as well. They cannot be separated.

And so, avoid undue affection for either the Cross or the Resurrection; do not presume to ignore either in favor of the other, for then you are quite lost, my brother – then you know neither the death of sin nor the glory of the Kingdom. Then you will be fooling yourself and attempting to make your own god. We must be baptized into His death to find new life. And we must find new life in His sacrifice.

2. Poverty

Having nothing. Wanting nothing. The LORD is my Shepherd, and so, what more could I want, what else do I need? He is all in all.

I encourage you to draw closer to this reality, my brother. In it is freedom, true freedom, absolute freedom from all worry and care. All is in God's hands – let it be so in your life.

This is how we come to Heaven; this is how Heaven comes to us: in poverty, in complete trust in the will of the LORD. In what else can we put our trust? All else will fail us.

Of course, people place their trust, even their lives, in money, in power, in honors... all the vain things of the world that sparkle with grand illusion. But they are indeed empty and lead nowhere, nowhere but back into the earth. It is Lazarus who was held in Abraham's bosom, he who had nothing in this world; he who was nothing in this world was everything in the eyes of God. This merits our contemplation.

How hard it is for us to realize that wealth and prestige will get us nowhere. How tightly we hold to such lies. On this earth they may provide us something, but whatever they provide will soon pass away. Will we pass away with them, or embrace poverty?

It is freedom your heart desires, brother, and this freedom can only be found in God and in giving all things over into His hands. True freedom is absolute surrender to the will of God, for only He is truly free: He holds all the world in His holy hands. (How wonderful it is to have nothing, for then everything is ours in the LORD.)

Paradox (III)

3. In Weakness

Scripture tells us that God's power is shown most perfectly in weakness, in our weakness, and His own.

Though seemingly paradoxical, it should be clear how God's power is shown in our weakness: it is when we are weak we need His power; and the weaker we are, the more we are in need of Him. And so when He acts in our lives, when He saves us from our weakness and brings us new strength, then we see clearly just how powerful He is.

Indeed, the weaker we are, the more His power is shown. It is like those forgiven their debts – the one who is forgiven more is more thankful to the LORD, for he is more aware of just how much grace has worked in his life; while he who is forgiven little has little sense of the grace and power of God.

But the power of God is also shown in *His* weakness, for in this is revealed His love, and there is nothing more powerful than the love of God. The Almighty LORD humbles Himself to walk among us; of this He is not ashamed. And not only does He take upon Himself our lowly form, He humbles Himself even to die on a cross, mocked and scourged like the worst of criminals.

How can He do this? How can He lower Himself so? And how does this reveal His power? Muslims and others see this as a scandal, as would anyone looking with the eyes of the world. But the LORD is not scandalized. His vision transcends that of His creatures, and His power is greater than anything we poor humans (or the angels) could inflict upon Him. It is because He is so great that He can endure this self-emptying and have His greatness, His perfection, remain unaffected… even as He places His arms around us and in His surpassing love redeems us from our sin. What more power could any being have?

4. Childlike

Another paradox: the most spiritually mature among us are the most childlike. Not childish, certainly, for how could they then be mature? But like children, as Jesus tells us we must be to enter the Kingdom of Heaven. For the wisdom of the child far surpasses the wisdom of any man – much as the Baptist was the greatest of men born of woman, yet he who is of the Kingdom is the greater blessed.

Could one who is not childlike believe in the Resurrection of the Christ? Would he not rather be trapped in numbers on a balance sheet and have his vision fixed to this earth? He could not look up; he could not see.... Would he not be utterly blind, my brother? Possessed by the things he seeks to possess, his breath would be taken from him – he wouldn't be able to live.

We must be set free from the bonds of this world! Of course, we must recognize the evils that abound and not be blind to that which is around us here – again, we cannot be childish. But without innocence, without purity, without the heart of a child that is in each of us, what good are we? We would be dead, indeed. We would remain blind to what is most true, what is most fundamental to our existence. It is not the stock market or the latest television show. It is the light of the LORD who made us, who breathes life into our souls.

We are made in His image, my friends. This we must know and remember. But unless we are as children, this truth will escape us, and we will know nothing at all.

5. Chastity

I have barely known Sister Chastity, and so I am barely qualified to speak of her: may she speak through me.

There is a purity, a purity that is of God, that embraces God, that is above this world and its corruption. People speak as if corruption by the flesh is inevitable; it is not. People think we are just animals unable to control our desires; we are not. There is a purity that embraces God (in marriage and in celibate life) and is above this world and its corruption, and it is native to every soul, if we would but embrace it.

Chastity is not a curse but a blessing, a tremendous blessing that brings us in touch with the angels – like angels we shall be on the last day (though always with bodies), and chastity enables us to taste that glory even here on earth. Indeed, it is what brings us from here to that place.

Chastity is a fruitful mother, the most fruitful of all... like our Blessed Mother, who though a Virgin has brought new life into the world, the new life of every soul. It is in Jesus chastity is found, and there, too, we find love.

Love is what the human heart most desires, what it most thirsts for, and what it most needs. Humans, especially in this age, confuse love with sex and so all sorts of troubles proceed. But it is love we need. And if we have that love, the love of Christ, then we are satisfied, we are happy... without it we will never find peace (neither here nor in Heaven), however much we seek.

6. Chastisement

We must be chastened; we must be made like God, and this cannot be done if we are not chastised for the sins each of us knows, that we might be purged of them. There is perhaps no greater grace than this chastisement (which indeed shows the love of God).

The first proclamation from the mouth of John the Baptist and from the Lord Himself is "Repent." The Kingdom of God is nigh unto us, particularly as Jesus has come to walk amongst us, and if we wish to enter therein, if we hope to unite ourselves with the Christ, we must indeed repent of our sins and be cleansed of them by the blood of that same Lamb. Else we shall remain apart from Him.

The light has come into the world, Jesus has come to save us, and we can accept His Word, His call to repent and come into that light… or remain in the darkness and condemnation our sins have brought upon us. This is our choice. The Lord is ready to receive us; He is seeking to chasten our hearts that they might be purified for the presence of God the Father – it is up to us to take the next step.

Do not turn from chastisement, my son; it is indeed the great love of the Father at work in your soul, in your life. Realize the great blessing it is and the place to which it brings you: you can be made ready to stand before the throne of the Almighty and be welcomed into His arms. O let this be the desire of your heart and the chastisement you will cherish!

Paradox (III)

7. Obedience

As difficult as poverty and chastity are for the modern mind to grasp, perhaps nothing escapes its understanding more than obedience, for man will do what he wants to do – and he calls this "freedom." But this is not freedom at all; it is but slavery to the passions, the body, as it were, ruling the spirit. This is the path to hell.

To bow before the wisdom of the Church seems like hell to many, for it would mean forgoing their addictions, the desires with which they have become so familiar. And so they will not listen – they will not obey. They will do as they please.

But what wisdom there is in obedience! What grace is upon the great saints who, like Ignatius, say that even if they see something as white, if the Church calls it black, it is black. Even those who possess ill will toward them they respect and love… and would kiss their hands.

"Insanity," the world says. "Do not humiliate yourself so. Stand up for your rights." There is, of course, nothing wrong with seeking justice; justice is a good…. But how much greater is the taste of suffering for what is right! And how much more effective a weapon it is.

The LORD has set a certain order to the universe and put men in positions of authority – and so the president and the bishop must be respected. It is not for us to question God's unfathomable will, but to accept it and so find the blessing contained therein. And the greatest blessing of all is freedom from our sinful inclinations, and humility as of the dust. But where is the man who can see this?

8. Peace

The paradox of peace. Most are familiar with the paradox Jesus presents when He, the Prince of Peace, says He has come not to bring peace but a sword. This paradox is easily understood if one simply contrasts the peace that exists in the Church, in the people of God, and the lack thereof present in the world. This contrast causes division between what is of the world and what is of God; thus the sword must come to divide the two, to separate evil from good.... But what of the paradox of war itself: is it simply another means of needed division, or should it be eliminated entirely?

Certainly in the end war will be entirely eliminated: the peace of the LORD will reign in His Kingdom – there will be no destruction on God's holy mountain. This is sure and is our sure hope. But what of this time, as the grass grows and men's hearts remain corrupt? What of this hour in which the devil still holds sway? Is there need for war in this state, or should Christians cast it away?

The Baptist did not tell the soldiers to leave their posts and Jesus held up the centurion as a model of faith, so it cannot be that armies are evil in and of themselves. The Lord seems to make allowance for war, and the Church teaches principles of a just war... but do we move toward a time when war should be set aside, a time when we must accept the Cross as has our Lord and insist that no man take up arms to defend us, however justified the cause? (And what could be more justified than fighting for the Christ? Yet Jesus insisted Peter lay down his sword.)

Whoever lives by the sword will die by the sword, and so we must not be of the sword. (How difficult this was for Peter to hear.) And St. Francis seems – with our recent Popes – to

Paradox (III)

lead us into an age when shield and sword are indeed set aside and there is no more need for any crusade. The time is nigh to truly embrace peace, a peace that can never be shaken (even by death itself).

9. Christian Warfare

We have already indicated how the peace of Christ is not the same as the peace the world gives, but let us more directly address the warfare Christians wage.

Christ came to die, He came to lay down His life – this was His entire mission, His essential purpose. He did battle against the devil by casting out demons and teaching with authority, but ultimately (and even in these other actions) He came to be crucified for our sins, to utterly defeat Satan by His death on the Cross.

Here is where glory is found, victory over sin and death: not on a battlefield where the goal is to kill, to take up arms against one's enemy and vanquish him... but to die, to lay down one's arms, and in this way to triumph.

This way of Christian warfare should not be so foreign to us, for we have seen it fought effectively in our own time by the likes of Mahatma Ghandi and Martin Luther King, who defeated the powers of oppression in this world by a willingness to suffer, a readiness to be beaten and even killed for their cause, employing a complete prohibition against taking up arms.

This same battle was fought at the exhortation of Pope St. John Paul the Great by the Solidarity movement in Poland, which was instrumental in dismantling Communism by peaceful means. And so with witnesses such as these, why should we question the wisdom of the call of Christ or hesitate to lay down our lives?

Do not be afraid. Do not be afraid to die for God, for truth, for peace, for love.... Be so filled with the love of God that nothing can dissuade you from following the path of the Cross. Have faith. There are many willing to kill, others or themselves, for their cause – where are those who are willing to die for the peace of Christ?

10. Doubt

What a crisis of faith exists today in the world and in the Church! So much doubt has been sown by souls readily set against the teachings of Christ and His Church, but also by many entrusted with their care. And so, what a crisis of faith exists today in the world and in the Church.

Doubt is hailed as a wonderful thing, much to be desired for the discovery of truth. But doubt itself inhibits truth as clouds inhibit the light of the sun. It is a work of darkness, of the devil, and is not to be nurtured by the Christian soul.

All are subject to doubt – this we do not doubt – just as all are subject to temptation. And such doubt cannot be ignored: we cannot pretend it does not exist (or that, too, would be a lie). Trials and temptations inevitably come, and they come especially to those seeking the LORD (but woe to those by whom they come). The key for the Christian is to turn the doubt back upon the devil and his minions by facing it and casting it away by exposing its lies.

Questions that arise in the soul must be asked. If we hide from them, they control us – they seek to make us hide in fear. But if we ask the questions openly, if we face the doubt in all

Paradox (III)

honesty and humility... then the truth will prevail and the doubt run like a frightened dog. And it will raise its head no more (for fear of having it cut off).

And facing the doubts that come (not manufacturing them) serves the great purpose of strengthening us in the faith. The darkness with which the devil would poison our souls is then indeed turned against him as an occasion for greater light. And how strong we may become in the LORD if we stand strong in the truth, never cowering to any lie (spoken by others or in our hearts), but taking our refuge in innocence.

11. Judgment

Judgment is mine, saith the LORD: judge not and you will not be judged. Let him without sin cast the first stone.... Yet how many stones are cast by those who presume to be Christian, and this with seeming impunity?

It is so, that in our lives we are called upon continually to make judgments; and we must decide aright, in accordance with the Word of God and the teaching of the Church. And continually we must beware the devil's trap of condoning the sins of others, or our own, out of a fear of being condemned as intolerant, out of a desire to be liked. We cannot be blind to the darkness all around us (and within us).

And so, how do we reconcile the Lord's clear proscription against judging and condemning with the need to discriminate against evil and for good? It should be evident that when Jesus commands us not to judge He is speaking of the condemnation of others' souls, of invoking a judgment as to their eternal damnation. Not even the Church is qualified to pronounce on this matter. (Thus she declares some persons saints and so in Heaven, but never that any particular soul is in hell.) And so we should *never* arrogate this power to ourselves, especially while we walk this soiled earth.

The cause of such unrighteous condemnation of others is often ignorance of our own sin – we are quick to justify our actions and condemn others'. But, again, we cannot ignore or condone sinful actions…. This is, in fact, where the line is drawn: we may with the wisdom and guidance of the LORD and His Church be called upon to denounce the sins that souls commit (including our own), but never can we condemn the souls themselves. It is with mercy we should always approach people in this world, with a heart that desires their turning away from evil to embrace God, with a desire thus for their salvation, never their condemnation. It should pain us to see others go astray.

12. Hate This World

Jesus' great command is the call to love, to love even as He has loved. It is He who reveals the love of the Father, who is Love. And yet He tells us that we must hate this world, hate even our own mother and father. How can this be?

So often intelligence, wisdom, is called for on the part of the Christian, on the part of all souls, and so often it is lacking. So often people are unable to think, to reason; particularly in this age of supposed higher education, common sense is severely missing. It seems sometimes that people understand nothing (though they think they know everything).

People think that when Jesus asks, "Who is my mother?" (i.e. the one who does the will of God), He is somehow

Paradox (III)

snubbing Mary. They cannot see that it is she who hears the Word of God and keeps it better than any creature that has ever lived. Jesus has only the greatest love for His Mother; certainly He keeps well the commandment to honor one's father and mother, and would insist upon every one of His followers doing the same. We must keep this in mind. It is certain that Jesus calls us to love *everyone*.

Thus when He says that whoever loves father and mother more than Him is not worthy of the Kingdom, He is not calling us to despise our parents but emphasizing that we must love Him first – God must always come first. (The things of the Spirit surpass those of the flesh.) And the souls who do possess intelligence, who seek and so are blessed with wisdom, realize that when we put God first, when Heaven is our priority, it is then that we can truly love all that God has made (including our parents). If we put anything before Him, we will not only be unable to love others, we will find that such disorder in our lives leads inevitably to hatred of those things we place before God... for they will thus keep us from the true love that is found only in Him and which all hearts desire. Purge your soul of all idols.

13. Adoration

Jesus is present in the Blessed Sacrament; God is with us here. This is the greatest gift He gives us on this earth, the gift of Himself and all the graces of His sacrifice. And so in this Sacrament we receive Him, and in this Sacrament we adore Him. Let all now fall before Him!

Yet when His Day comes this Sacrament shall be no more, for we shall not need it any longer. As marvelous as it is for our journey to the Kingdom, once we arrive at that Kingdom, it shall no longer be. But He will be. He will be all in all.

And so in this sense the Sacrament never ends, never leaves us at all. The altar and the host will be gone, but He remains, and in a complete manner – absolute fulfillment of His Presence will be known. One can thus say that the Sacrament will be everywhere, insofar as it is Jesus, the LORD, God, who makes the Sacrament what it is: all that shall happen is the removal of the veil that we might see Him face to face.

Then our adoration will also be complete. Here we must adore Him, here we are able to know Him and praise Him present on our altars and in our tabernacles (and in us)… but O what praise shall resound in His Holy Kingdom! From end to end His praise shall ring out from the heart of every creature. Then we shall be enveloped in His Light. Then our joy will indeed be complete. And now in this Sacrament we may begin to taste this joy.

14. Time

Time. And eternity. Time stretches out like the continents across the earth. We measure it with the rising and setting sun and the phases of the moon. We trace it to minutes and seconds with our clocks and watches…. But does it really move at all?

Certainly people grow older, their bodies break down – there is change that occurs (after the Fall) in the physical universe. And time is associated with this; it measures it in the passing of days and years (and centuries). But at the

Paradox (III)

center of time and space is a still point, where no time passes, where God the Creator of all makes His home.

The LORD is far beyond time, outside of the universe… but He is also as the axis upon which the world spins, and His presence at the heart of all has been made known in the Incarnation of His Son. And so, eternity enters time, shows itself to be its source.

There would be no time without eternity, without the timeless, just as there would be no words without the silence of the LORD, without His NAME speaking in all. All would be but sound and fury; all would be chaos, and we would not know even the chaos, for then there would be only destruction, only death… nothing at all.

The Light of Christ separates us from the yawning darkness and gives us time, time to set our hearts aright – it gives us a chance to find the timeless, to find the LORD present at the heart of all. But if we waste this time, of what use is it? If we do not enter eternal life, we shall soon die. And such death will not be nothing; for now we have had time to discover God, and failing that only purpose worthy of existence, the repercussions will haunt us beyond time. (Call now upon the LORD your God.)

IV

1. Three in One

The Holy Trinity is at the very heart of our faith – it is in the Name of the Father, and of the Son, and of the Holy Spirit we are baptized and so enter the Church, and so enter upon the path to salvation. This is our foundation and it must be strong in order to be built upon.

But who can understand the Trinity? How can there be three Persons in one God? Muslims accuse us of worshiping multiple gods and so being no better than the pagans. It would, of course, contradict the very essence of our faith if this were true, for above all we believe that God is One. (Ours is the same God Moses proclaimed, the same God of Abraham, Isaac, and Jacob.) And so we cannot be Catholic, cannot be Christian, if we believe in more than one God. Yet how can we keep from getting confused, as others do, by our firm belief in Three Persons?

I will not attempt proofs of the Trinity, but I will say that one must come from a starting point of faith even to begin to fathom the greatness of our God and His essence. Muslims are right to say that the LORD is far beyond our understanding, immaterial and eternal, all-powerful and all-knowing.... But God is something more than this: He is all-loving, too. And if one is willing to meditate on His love, one may begin to recognize His Three Persons.

Could God not become Man and walk amongst us? Is this beyond the ability of the all-powerful LORD? And if He did so, would He cease to be God? More importantly, would we deny Him the power to love, to love beyond the capability of

Paradox (IV)

any human being? And so, could He not willingly lay down His life for the sake of His children, for the sake of those whom He loves? Is it not thus He comes among us? Finally, would He not in His love wish us to share eternity with Him in His presence?

To oneness He invites us, to share in the oneness of the Father and the Son, and the Spirit that is their love.

2. Light

Some people, not thinking very clearly, ask how Light could be the LORD's first creation and yet the sun and stars not be made until the fourth day – and in their own confusion they accuse the Bible of being confused. (This confusion of the Light of God with the light of the sun might be excusable in those not conversant with the Word of God, but one wonders at the lack of wisdom in those who profess to be scholars of the Word.)

The Light of God is not dependent on the light of the sun; the light of the sun is but a pale reflection of the divine Light that illumines the heart of every man and the universe itself. Have you not read that in the Kingdom there will be no need for sun or moon or lamp of any kind, but that the LORD Himself will give light to all? Do you think that when David sings of the LORD being "wrapped in light as in a robe," it is the light of lamp or sun of which he speaks? Is it this light that shone from Jesus at the Transfiguration? Could anyone with sense be this blind?

Those without the Spirit of God, and so without His Light, grope blindly in the dark, unable to see what is plain as day. They have no light and so they cannot see – it is this simple.

Those who are blessed by the Holy Spirit and filled with His Light have not only faith in the LORD of all but also the intelligence to comprehend the things of this world: it is only they who have sense. Thus it says in the Word of God that the Prodigal Son "came to his senses" – with his repentance came a certain intelligence that made clear to him how absurd his life had become, and how easy was the way home. (I pray the Light of the Spirit upon you, my son.)

3. Prophecy

How little seems to be understood of prophecy even by those who should best understand it. Prophecy is little understood because faith is lacking; in some ways it is almost non-existent. The cloud that blocks the faith of Christians also blinds their understanding of prophecy.

It is a secular, materialistic world in which we live, and how it swallows those who are not diligently on guard against its grasp. Indeed, it reaches even into the Church and breeds a complacency that stultifies souls, again, even those addressed as scholars. And so when certain theologians speak, they speak not prophetically of the Word of God or the teaching of the Church – they speak with a voice colored by the world and its secularist influence. To this influence they genuflect in fear.

And so, fear of God is replaced by fear of offending the status quo, the popular beliefs of those who hold sway. And so, where is prophecy? If God is eliminated, prophecy has no place, for prophecy is His voice. But to this voice no one listens, and with this voice no one speaks.

Paradox (IV)

But though the Word of God may be lost even by some authorities in the Church, it does not cease to exist; it does not stop speaking – the voice of the LORD indeed fills the earth. And for those who desire and so find moments of clarity amongst the din of vain chatter, it speaks profoundly: it leads them to the presence of God. And there the Lord Jesus reveals the NAME of the Father, there the Spirit breathes His Silence… and so they are able to speak, to speak of that which the world would silence. They speak of the glory and wonder of our God and His work in faithful souls. He is LORD, now and forever.

4. Parables

The parables of Jesus are a clear sign of the paradoxical nature of the Christian faith, not just in their message (the last shall be first, etc.), but in the parables themselves; for they are not limited to what they *say*: their meaning goes beyond the words.

Jesus makes the paradoxical nature of His parables very evident when He says that people will listen to them but not hear them, that their meaning will completely escape them because they have "eyes to see but see not and ears to hear but hear not." How can one have ears and yet not hear (though one is not deaf) or eyes to see and not see…? Indeed the sound touches their ears and they could repeat the words spoken, but in the words they lose themselves and so come not to the Spirit.

The unenlightened mind, the soul not set on the things of Heaven but on those of earth, hears of seeds and ground and the growth of grain and thinks only of seeds and ground and the growth of grain – he can see no more than what appears to be there. And seeing only this, he cannot turn to be healed of his blindness... because he cannot see it. O how trapped he is in his sin!

What shall save him? What shall bring this soul from darkness to light? Only the grace of the Holy Spirit, only the will of the Father and the blood of the Son... and only if this is what he desires. Else the devil will continue to take the Word of God from him even as it touches his eardrums. (It shall never reach his heart.)

O LORD, give us ears to hear and eyes to see; give us a heart set on you and your love. Leave us not alone, deaf and blind as any stone or beast of the field, but be the light of our eyes and soften our hearts to your Word that calls us beyond what we see and hear into your holy Presence. Help us grow closer to you.

5. Here and Everywhere

There is no place the LORD is not, and yet He is contained by no place, for He is everywhere... and far beyond here. The LORD is present to me now as I write this, and He is present to you as you read it, whenever you read, whatever time you are in. And if many people read this at many different times and in many different places, He is with them everywhere they are. And He is with those who do not read this while others do, and present to all who are not writing with me now.

He is here and everywhere, at this time and at all times, and exists far beyond time, for He is eternal. Without beginning or end either in time or in space, He yet contains all

Paradox (IV)

time and space while not being contained by it at all. All-encompassing is our God. (And would you put your finger on Him?)

Thus, if we come to be where He is – as we are called – then we too will be everywhere at all times, though only by participation in His eternal glory and not by our own power or in our own nature. On that Day, time as we know it will pass away and be no more, and the heavens and the earth will be rolled up like a scroll and cease to be as well. But we shall not cease to be, if we are with Him, if in Him who is eternal and omnipresent we make our home.

Let us join the angels and saints in the eternal Kingdom of God; let us live and breathe in His light and His Spirit. He is with us even now. Remember: He is everywhere.

6. Ineffable

The LORD we cannot know or understand or comprehend. He is ineffable. His NAME best reveals His ineffability, for it is pronounceable silence. Thus only by recognizing His ineffability, only by realizing that He is beyond our understanding, do we come to know the LORD.

As the Divine NAME silences our tongues and so brings us into the presence of God, so when we silence our minds and our wills we begin to approach His majesty, His glory. As long as we think we can grasp Him on our own, His presence will elude us (much to our detriment).

Bow down before the glory of the LORD! Bend your knee at the Silence of His NAME! You are but a creature, His creation, and would you presume to stand before Him and defend yourself? Would you presume to approach Him with words? Your mouth will soon return to dust, and with this would you confront the One who lives forever?

May your mouth be left agape in the presence of the LORD; then you will be blessed, then you will know what you could never know by your own power. In such humility you will find your place; in such silence the heavens will speak. Then you may be inspired to sing with the angels of the surpassing glory of the One God and Father of all.

Do not forget His ineffability; do not forget His NAME. Remember always how far beyond us is the LORD and His ways, and into His ways you may be drawn... and of His glory you might speak.

7. The Whole Law

Under the Covenant of old it was said to violate the smallest letter of the law was to violate the whole law – thus the impossibility of keeping the old law. None could do so but the Christ, who was perfect in Himself, the Word and the Law Himself, and so the fulfillment of the law.

But see what keeping the whole law means, where it leads: to the Cross, to crucifixion of the Son of God. In no other way could the law be fulfilled than with the sacrifice of the Son. And the only way we ourselves can keep the law is by joining in His sacrifice – this is where the law, the Law of love, leads all souls.

Now here is the paradox: we cannot keep the whole law; we sin against the law of God, against His love (for the law is summed up in love), even if only in the smallest of ways. And if only in the smallest of ways we sin against the LORD,

Paradox (IV)

the whole law comes down upon us. Now, is this a curse for the Christian, or a blessing?

It is a blessing for us insofar as it thus allows us to join in the sacrifice of Christ – and so, paradoxically, to fulfill the whole law. There may be those among us who might become self-satisfied with their state, with the progress they have made, and therefore begin to think they no longer need the forgiveness of Jesus, that they can no longer benefit from His blood. Such thoughts would separate us from the love of Christ, from His sacrifice, and bring us to a pitiful place.

This the saints know very well. This is how those closest to the Lord can see themselves as those furthest from Him and not be wrong, and not simply be imagining things: the smallest of sins they commit grants them entry into comprehension and experience of the greatest sins committed by men (for indeed sinning in small things brings the whole law upon us), and thus they can identify with Christ on the Cross, able to offer their own lives for the sins of others and so approach fulfillment of the whole law. What a joy this is for the truly Christian soul!

8. Glorified

Now is the Son of Man glorified, now that He takes up His Cross – even as night falls the brightest of light comes. This is how He turns the wiles of Satan back upon him.

With every blow, every tear of Jesus' skin, every wound in His head, His hands, His feet, His side – with every violent strike of the devil, the glory of God becomes known… and souls are released from their prison.

Two Books

This is how it occurs, the salvation of mankind; this is how we are brought to glory (with Him): in His suffering and death, in His crucifixion – in the Passion He undergoes for our sake. His words prepare our hearts to receive such a blessing, His healing makes us ready to believe it shall be so… but it is His sacrifice that fulfills His mission, that effects the salvation of our souls.

O what a paradox is here! For most horrible is the torture He endures; most grievously should we mourn the death of the Son. Yet how gloriously we should sing His praises; how greatly we should celebrate the graces that pour upon us with every blow – indeed, in this way He makes all things new.

And the glory cannot be separated from the terrible punishment He readily endures. And so, we cannot despair (as He cannot despair) when the persecution is upon Him, for we know, as He knew, the Paradise to which His sacrifice leads. He is buoyed by the blessing He brings us, and we should take that blessing upon ourselves. (O to be forever in His glory!)

9. You Are My Tabernacle

O Lord, how can I be your tabernacle as you call me to be, as you call all Christians to be – for as Paul has told us, we are temples of the Holy Spirit – as is your Mother, who is the Ark of the Covenant with whom you always dwell (even as you assured her in the temple when she thought she had lost you)?

Your Mother is your Mother, kept from sin all her life and in whom you were conceived and carried to birth… and who indeed remains with you always in your Kingdom. How can

Paradox (IV)

we be as she? How can we have you always with us; how can we be so holy?

We cannot, and yet we must. We carry your blessings in earthen vessels so subject to the distractions and snares of this world. This world is indeed an unholy place, falling far short of your glory, and it is here we yet live and move.... Your tabernacles exist only in your churches, which are set aside as your House, as the place where you repose – how can we really be as your Temple?

We cannot, and yet we must. And so it is only by your grace it can be done at all, only by your grace we can even begin to approach such a call. Help us not to get in the way.

O may we carry you wherever we go! Let it be in us you make your home. Let us not forget the blessing we receive in Holy Communion, and in kneeling before your Presence on the altar. We are your tabernacles. You come within us with your own Body and Blood. Let it be your blood that courses through our veins; let our flesh be of your flesh, our bone of your bone. By your grace let this be done. (And may your Mother help us.)

10. To What Is Above

St. Paul exhorts us to set our hearts on what is above, where Jesus is seated (not on the earth, where snakes slither); and so it is that we must turn our minds from the things around us to attain to Heaven, to become, as it were, tabernacles of the LORD. But most of all what is needed is grace to fall upon us from God's throne.

What is above comes to us here below and draws us up into the presence of the LORD. We can, and we must, prepare our hearts to receive such grace – by Baptism, regular reception of Holy Communion, regular Confession, constant prayer... but it is not by our own power we shall enter the LORD's presence: it must come from Him. And He touches whom He will when He will, and there is no determining when this will be. Some may seek holiness many years and not receive His touch for many years more, while others may receive it more immediately. It is indeed in God's hands. But when it comes, it is His hand that reaches down to us to draw us unto Heaven.

But one must confirm that it is not *only* grace that is involved in this blessing. We have already said that we must do what we can do, and our prayers and good works certainly prepare us for the day of His coming. (And the more we pray, the more patience we find, so that when the moment comes it will seem a very short time.) The grace of the LORD must be met with our acceptance, our willingness to rise to what is above with Him, or it will be fruitless for us.

In the end He needs but the slightest movement of the heart, a glance above our situation with a readiness to leave behind our own weakness (and the weakness we see in others). It is in a breath, the beat of a heart turned toward Him.... Really, His Word (His NAME) at the center of our being is what draws us there, and is our means to Him as well. (Might I call it a silence at the center of our skulls that raises our heads to what is above?)

11. Suffering and Joy...

A priest tells the story of a time during his formation when a fellow seminarian became very ill, his disease causing

Paradox (IV)

emaciation and bringing him near death. The last time he visited his friend in the hospital, he found him in the arms of his mother. His friend called him closer and, barely able to speak, whispered in the priest's ear: "You can't believe the joy!" Can you believe the joy that comes through suffering with Christ?

It is an essential question and call of Christianity and yet one we all have difficulty understanding and answering with full voice. It is indeed through suffering that joy comes – this is the lesson of the Cross... and it is a joy to behold.

I struggle to embrace the Cross as all do, and most often am far from realizing this great gift, but I recall speaking to a professor after class once – having just discussed the subject with regard to St. Catherine of Siena – and the absolute truth that joy and suffering *cannot be separated*, that they are *one*, overwhelmed me, and at that moment I understood it perfectly.

But that moment was passing. And though there have been other moments like it, though I can remember, for instance, on a retreat once praying the Stations united with Christ in a clear joy even as I bore His Cross... moments like this have also been passing – and the grasping of this truth in anything approaching a complete manner continues to escape me.

But I know this is truth. And I know this is a paradox we all must realize: there is no joy without suffering as there is no Resurrection without the Cross. May the LORD bless us all with full understanding and comprehension of this profound truth of the Faith.

12. Pray in Secret

The Lord instructs His disciples to go into their rooms to pray, for the Father is hidden and it is in secret we find Him. We should not parade our prayer on street corners, seeking the adulation of others... yet Jesus also tells us our light must shine forth for others to see: a lamp is not hidden under a bushel basket.

So how do we reconcile the need to pray in secret with the call to proclaim the Word of God to all? It should not be difficult to decipher, but unfortunately can be for those lacking wisdom.

The Lord's word against praying in public is a warning against pride; that should be clear. If we seek and receive recognition from others, we can expect none from God, for He has a heart only for the humble. Whatever we do we must be selfless in our actions, as Jesus Himself – pride has no place in a Christian's life.

Jesus' exhortation to shine our light forth for the world to see is likewise a call to lay down our lives. We should not be concerned with praise from others or even with their thanks, but as we do the work of the Lord have a heart set on the good of others and do all for their sakes. The same selflessness applies.

One thing we should understand (so as not to get trapped on the surface of things and thus become lost in superficiality) is that when Jesus speaks of going into our room, He means our heart (where God dwells). Wherever we are and whenever we pray (and we must "pray always"), we must pray in our hearts, or our prayer is vain. Whether in our homes or in church or on a street corner (or subway car), we must commune with the LORD at the center of our souls for our prayer to be fruitful.

And when we act, in speech or in deed, thus serving to share the LORD's light in the world, likewise our actions must come from our hearts, from our place of prayer, or they too will be nothing worth.

13. I Do Not Know

I suppose we have touched upon this before, perhaps even several times, but it strikes me as most important to make clear note of the great significance of recognizing our lack of knowledge of God in order to begin to know Him.

It is a simple thing, really, as simple as God Himself: the LORD is unknowable, and if we recognize this essential truth, then truly do we begin to know Him. It sounds like I am talking in circles and creating paradox, but that is the way the simplest things often seem. Let me try to state it again: if we acknowledge that God is unknowable, then we are recognizing this basic truth about Him (that He is unknowable). What follows after is the grace of the LORD at work – for once we admit our inability to know Him, once we confess how small we are and how beyond us He is, then with this basic truth present in our souls He takes us in His loving hands and raises us up from our ignorance (by His grace) to begin to understand the wonder and glory of Who He Is... though we can never grasp it all. (The truth indeed sets us free!)

And the more we recognize and admit our ignorance, our smallness, our humility before Him... the more He fills our minds with knowledge, our hearts with love, our bodies with strength, and our souls with His presence – the more He becomes a part of us, taking pity on our poverty and filling us with His riches. For our innocence and desire for Him He cannot resist.

Say to Him repeatedly, "I do not know you, LORD" and then say it again (and ever again); say it with a desire to know Him in your heart and He will reveal Himself to you. And your spirit shall become one with His own.

14. Beyond the Law

The Lord calls us beyond the law inscribed in stone to the Law of love He writes upon our hearts. He tells His disciples their faith must exceed that of the Pharisees if they are to enter the Kingdom of Heaven, for that Kingdom is of love and nothing short of the love of God can enter there. Thus one could indeed call one's brother to task for being angry; thus one's tongue and the words that flow therefrom become as significant as one's actions. Thus we cannot simply say we haven't killed anyone, for the LORD reads our hearts and knows our thoughts, and by these, too, we are judged. And we owe no debt except to love.

The letter of the law must be followed: the LORD will not countenance any breaking of His Word to Moses. So we must never use Jesus' call to go beyond the law as excuse to go, as it were, below the law by taking it in our own hands and choosing which precepts we will follow or not. Again, the LORD will countenance no breaking of His commandments (as expressed through His Church). We cannot rise above the law by ignoring it but only by fulfilling it and going beyond it

Paradox (IV)

in our practice of the faith, in our practice of God's love. (And this we can do only by God's grace.)

The demands Jesus makes upon us are far greater than the demands of the old law, for, as we have indicated, nothing imperfect, nothing falling short of God's all-embracing love, will enter His Kingdom; and Jesus wants very much for us to enter that Kingdom. Those who make excuses for the sins of others, however small (thus condoning and encouraging them), do not show compassion for their neighbors but an indifference regarding their souls. It is Jesus who is compassionate, who truly cares for all, and thus does He call us to perfection in Him; for, indeed, He would have us with Him in eternal life (which is a life far greater than that of this world).

V

1. The Paradox of Paul

The letters of Paul are filled with paradox, and he himself is a tremendous paradox: the great persecutor of Christ and His Church become the great Apostle of both. Of course he speaks well of the joy that comes through suffering, for he suffered so much – trials and beatings and stonings and shipwrecks and terrible anxiety for those in his care (and finally, beheading)... and experienced so much joy as a result.

We see this sense of rejoicing for being worthy of the persecutions of Christ in the apostles who are chastised and beaten at the hands of the Sanhedrin for persistently giving witness to the Lord; and this same joy in following the way of Jesus is known by all of His disciples, even to this day... but Paul seems particularly exemplary in the paradoxes that characterize his life and his teaching.

He witnesses well to the Corinthians, for instance, how he and those with him are thought of as nothing and no one, yet they are – and we know this now more than he could have been aware at the time – well known throughout the world for the great work they accomplish in Jesus' Name. They have nothing and yet they possess everything, for all the world is the Lord's and they are His ambassadors. These outcasts for the Name of Christ are those who rule with Him in the Kingdom of God... and that Kingdom is now brought to bear even in this place.

So if anyone should want to understand what great paradox there is in being Christian, let him carefully read St. Paul's letters. They should be especially instructive. And call

Paradox (V)

upon his intercession to follow in that way; be imitators of him as he is of Christ (who has called us always to turn the other cheek).

2. Be Perfect

This is the instruction of the Lord, and it is a most solemn one. We must be like our Heavenly Father, who is perfect. This is as Jesus is and we must be the same. Perfect. But how can sinners like us answer such a call? Does Jesus not speak of an impossibility?

Jesus does not offer solemn instruction in vain; He does not speak intently about things that cannot be. He means what He says, always, but especially when He proffers wisdom as significant as this command.

And this is a command. He is not *suggesting* that we be perfect, He is telling us to be perfect; for, again, He wants what is best for us and there is nothing better for us than to share in the glory of God the Father.

So it is a goal that is attainable, nay, one that is *necessary* for us to achieve. But the question remains: how can sinners such as we are attain to such a lofty goal? How can we live and breathe in the light of the LORD, becoming even as His only Son?

It is impossible. It is impossible, and until we see that this is something impossible for us to achieve on our own, we will never even begin to move toward it. We must recognize, and without equivocation, without excuse, that we are sinners who are an infinity from the glory of God. It is impossible for us even to imagine becoming one with the LORD.

Two Books

But once we do admit our weakness, our sinfulness in the sight of God – that we fall infinitely short of His glory – then His grace can begin to work in us and draw us to Him. But it must be something we desire, something we recognize as a good: to be like Him, to love like He does…. To pray even for our enemies should not be a labor we dread but a call we celebrate for its bringing us into the presence of the LORD and making us as He is.

We must want to be like Him, and be willing to sacrifice to find Him, and His glory will be upon us.

3. Justice and Mercy

There is much controversy about the relationship of justice and mercy, especially as it concerns the LORD. His justice and mercy are one and the same (as is all in Him), for His mercy is perfect justice and His justice perfect mercy. One could not separate them with the sharpest of sword s.

Look upon the Cross. See our Savior hanging there. Here is mercy, perfect mercy; and here is the justice of the LORD fulfilled. You need look no further to see the Hand of God at work.

His arms are open to all – there is none upon whom His blood does not fall. And so His mercy is complete. And all our sins are gathered there (and fix Him to the wood) – there is nothing for which He fails to atone. And so to the letter His justice clears the ledger.

Do you require further explanation? Do you still see contradiction between the two? Then you are not looking clearly upon His corpus; then you need to take up the Cross yourself. In any who walk in His way no question remains.

Paradox (V)

So learn to bleed in His stead and you will see with heavenly vision.

By mercy justice is fulfilled as surely as the sacrifice of Christ removes all our sin. What could fulfill the absolute justice of God but this holy offering of His Son? And where could greater mercy be known than in the blood He freely shed?

Drink of His blood; see His light shine. All becomes clear in the shadow of His Cross and the glory to which it leads.

4. The Rosary

Some see the Rosary as the multiplicity of words our Lord warns against, since the prayers are continually repeated. A few enter freely into the meditation called for in each decade (and so draw close to the mystery of salvation they address), but many more, I fear, struggle in their attentiveness and tend to fall into the mouthing of words.

Now St. Louis de Montfort has indicated well how even just the speaking of the words is a positive force, a prayer with some fruit, because the words do proclaim the salvation of the Lord and our need to worship Him. (Suppose words praising Satan were spoken instead; as the saint tells us, even if said without much thought, still this would constitute an unholy practice with negative consequences.)

Certainly the Rosary is not meant to stop at the speaking of the words, with mouthing sounds (like some kind of parrot), but consider the words themselves: ironically, the prayer Jesus instructs His disciples to pray (immediately after warning against mounting up words!) is that which is the keynote of the Rosary: the Our Father, or the Lord's Prayer. So to this extent we are following our Savior's guidance.

As for the Hail Mary, the other essential part of the Rosary (and the prayer repeated most often), one should keep in mind that the words contained therein also come from the gospels, and are particularly inspired by the Holy Spirit: the Angel's greeting and call of Mary, Elizabeth's declaration of her blessedness, and Mary's own proclamation of the LORD's grace upon her. These are not just any words we say, and they do not come from our own conceit. (The same is true for our invocation of this Saint of saints' intercession for our sakes.)

The words should be prayed with concentration and commitment, with faith in what we speak; and we should certainly do our best to meditate on the mysteries they present, and so enter as best we can into the LORD's presence. But certainly there is no patent emptiness to this blessed prayer. It can indeed be a grace-filled means to deeper conversion toward Christ.

Let all who pray it, pray it well: pray it from the heart.

5. Martyrdom

Those who die for the Faith. Who are they? Why do they do it? Why should they be so honored? Are they not denying the life God gave them?

A martyr is one who loves life more than anyone and has a clear grasp of the beauty and wonder of life; and he knows that life exists in God alone. He does not reject this life – for indeed it is made by God and was blessed by Him – but sees

Paradox (V)

more deeply into the nature of life and its goodness... and seeks a greater share.

God is in this world. By His Breath this world was made and by His Breath it is sustained – it would quickly pass away without His love. And so, every Christian soul must treasure the life he has been given and the grace it is from the hand of the LORD. A martyr's death is never anti-life.

But how much can one love one's life? This is the question. One cannot love one's life more than God Himself, who gave us life. One cannot put the things that are less than God ahead of Him who is to be most greatly treasured. But, still, one must love one's life with all one's heart, mind, soul, and strength. And this is martyrdom – this is being fully alive in God.

A martyr is one who loves so much that he lives only for God, and so is always ready to die for Him as well. He knows the offering of his life is the greatest gift he can give, and so he holds nothing back for himself.

This is truly and completely embracing life. And the life he embraces shall not escape him: he will never die, never be separated from the One he loves, who is Life itself and holds all the good things of this life in His hands as well. (And so, neither from them shall the martyr be separated.)

In life and in death, lay down your life – we are all called to be martyrs for the LORD, witnesses to His love.

6. Stewards of Creation

The LORD has put this earth into the hands of men to care for and cultivate. Though they must in a sense conquer it to make it fruitful, they cannot abuse such a gift, for it is the Creation of God.

So many people see contradiction here: it is man's to use and master; it must be taken in hand with great care. There should be no opposition in these two points, yet how many make war over them!

What is the point of mastering the earth if we destroy it in the process? Can that in any real sense be called mastery? It is rather a kind of plundering. Mastering the earth must entail making it fruitful, helping it to feed well the needs of those who depend on it for their livelihood. There is not a man alive not dependent upon the earth for his survival, and his flourishing, and so to destroy it is to destroy ourselves (and all the other creatures as well).

Yet caring for the earth can in no way serve to diminish man and his inherent dignity; it cannot condemn him who is its steward, as if that which is in his care is of greater worth than him who cares for it. What good is an earth that nourishes no one? It immediately loses its purpose and falls into ruin.

The earth needs man and man needs the earth – this fact is undeniable. And so the two cannot be pitted against one another but *must* work in harmony; for the two truly are united and dependent upon one another.

Let us turn to the LORD to teach us how to be stewards of His Creation, never raping the Sister, the Mother, He has placed in our care, but rather nurturing her by the wisdom the LORD imparts, that she might share her fruits with all made from her.

Paradox (V)

7. To Flee or To Fight

The LORD calls Lot out of Sodom as He is about to destroy it for its grave depravity. Jesus instructs His disciples to leave Jerusalem before its time of destruction. We cannot remain in a city that has sunk decisively into immorality, that has so refused obedience to the voice of God that it can no longer remain on the face of the earth (even for its own sake). And so when we see the darkness closing in on our society, we must go.

But the LORD also calls us to shine our light in the darkness, to be as a lamp in a dark place, for the world is corrupt and Christians are like stars in the night sky. We must beware throwing our pearls before swine, it is true... yet we must proclaim the Word of God to all the world. The question is how to resolve these contrasting thoughts and commands.

We must go as the LORD directs us, and we must listen carefully and dispassionately for His voice, not leaning toward staying or going, not relying on our own will and wants, but desiring to fulfill His call.

And so, what should we do now that the United States has sunken into such depths that it celebrates and institutionalizes grave sin, thus legitimizing it and encouraging souls on the path to hell? Is it time to flee? Or is there yet hope that we can fight, that we can evangelize and overcome the darkness by our witness to the nation?

I do not have an answer to this question; it seems the darkness is complete... but there are those who still stand against the tide. Each day and at every moment we must wait on the LORD's command, on His blessed guidance, remaining in His presence ready to go as He instructs.

8. Radiant Disappointment

The LORD can work in the most disappointing and tragic events of our life, turning them into opportunities for grace. This is essentially the Cross, of course, of which we have spoken much: in the Cross the greatest tragedy becomes the greatest victory. And I have witnessed elsewhere that in my own life the greatest tragedy (the death of my younger sister at an early age) was the source of the greatest blessing (my reconversion to the Faith). But it needs for us to bring this truth onto an everyday level, so that we may be able to recognize the hand of God at work even in seemingly mundane things and learn to take those that appear only to be disappointing, mistaken or otherwise accompanied by a wish they had never happened, and find in them the ray of light, the triumph of the LORD... and through them come to greater blessing. Essentially this means embracing the Cross day to day and hour to hour.

How easy it is to curse the darkness, to regret the negative occurrences in our lives, and how inclined we are to do so. It is only natural, I suppose; but the life of a Christian is more than a natural life – it must be infused with the light of God and bring about a renewal of our minds. And so, that wrong turn we take when travelling on an unfamiliar road may not be a mere delay in our well-made plans but a correction of them by a Mind that can see the path ahead far better than we. And so it might lead us to a better place, a graced opportunity... or keep us from some dire consequence.

How can we learn to see with eyes that welcome whatever comes, finding in all circumstances the hand of God in our lives and turning all into light? We must be patient, certainly, and humble. We must first set ourselves on the will of God

Paradox (V)

and be ready to be moved by His Word. Overall, we must have faith and let our minds be infused with His wisdom. He always leads us to the Kingdom.

9. Pastoral Truth

It seems a difficult question: how does one remain pastoral – whether one is a pastor or not – and yet clearly profess the truth of doctrine? How does one keep one's humor, that is, remain human, kind, understanding of others' situations and empathetic toward them, while providing any necessary correction and not compromising the teaching of the Church?

The apparent contradiction in approaches can seem so great that it can create a warlike division among peoples. But this contradiction, though it takes patience and humility to resolve, is in essence a false dichotomy. It is most necessary for any pastor or priest, and indeed anyone in a position of guiding others (parents, teachers, even friends and relatives) to speak the truth in love. This is the simple, basic call of every Christian and must guide us in all we do.

If we fail to speak the truth, we fail as Christians – we oppose Christ who is the Truth. But Jesus is also the Way, and if we fail to present the truth with love, we likewise fail, for above all, God is Love. Both are absolutely necessary if we are to be authentic Christians.

We cannot fall into judgment or condemnation of those we perceive as sinning against the truth, against the teaching of the Faith; nor of those we see as sinning against love. For then we ourselves would be sinners, no better than the souls we presume to condemn (and thus condemn ourselves). We must love others and we must speak the truth to them. Love *and* truth or nothing at all. That is the bottom line.

But for those more inclined to defend the truth than act in love, a certain patience will be needed: we must nurture in our hearts a genuine love of those who may stray. Approach fellow weak humans understanding well how easy it is to fall into error or sin (be it anger, lust, greed, or whatever might be one's particular weakness). And as for those more inclined to love than to teach the truth, we must watch that we do not lead others astray or condone wrong action in any way. If we truly care about them, we will guide them into the light.

10. Peacemakers

How necessary are peacemakers in the world and in the Church, people who stand in the breach between enemies plagued by irrational fear and resolve differences with patience and truth. It is the call of the Christian, the call to lay down our lives to aid those in need; and those embroiled in hatred of their neighbor are among those most in need.

Here we find Christian paradox take human form, in the making of peace between those of flesh and blood by those of flesh and blood. In this peacemaking, contradiction is really overcome... and a sense of the Kingdom breathes upon those who find such peace.

The LORD is of peace – this we must know first of all. Though His Word brings division between those who embrace it and those who reject it, He Himself is only Peace (much as He is only Love) and He invites others only to His peace. And so, from this foundation of peace the peacemaker

Paradox (V)

must work: he must always maintain the LORD's peace within his soul.

In such a state he is able to reach out to warring factions and objectively weigh their concerns, confirming those which are authentic and shining the light of truth upon those that reveal a selfish preoccupation or, indeed, irrationality. He can thus encourage both sides to take an honest look at themselves, and at their opponents.

The peacemaker is always ready to die for the sake of bringing peace, and it is in seeing this that the warring parties become convinced of the peacemaker's genuine concern for each of them; and in turn they are able to confront their shortcomings in a direct manner, no longer afraid to admit their own guilt or to forgive the guilt the other. Thus does peace come.

11. Power

Jesus has all power in Heaven and on earth, yet how is that power put into effect and what is its source? How does Jesus, and how should His disciples, understand and employ power?

There are those of the world who lord it over souls in their care, who wield power like a blunt instrument to beat their servants into submission. These take pride in their power, exalting themselves over those under their dominion. But this is not power as preached and lived by Christ, and this power will not last; it shall be exposed for all the evil it holds, and those who wield it will retreat in shame from the presence of the all-powerful LORD and God.

Two Books

No, the power of God is founded in humility and centered on service to others. We have certainly touched upon this point before (and likely shall again) because it is essential to the way of Christ. Indeed, Jesus, who is one with the Almighty God, who is God Himself, came to serve and not to be served; He came to lay down His life for all. And this must be the attitude of those who would follow in His way and bear the name of Christian.

Our hearts must be set on service of others; and when they are, the LORD will entrust us with the power only He holds. If we recognize the power is not our own but comes as a gift from Him for the sake of the Church and the world, then that power will be increased for us, for then it will be properly employed. The LORD indeed desires for us to bear fruit in His Name, not to be unproductive or waste our talents in any way, and so when in humility we serve as He calls, He will increase our yield a hundredfold.

O LORD, send us souls that will teach and govern in your Name and in your Spirit, that all your children may be blessed.

12. Beauty

Shall I speak of beauty? It seems something modern man has forgotten, so preoccupied with utility as he is. So it matters no longer to him how things are but only what profit he can gain from them. And this utilitarian attitude, this objectification of reality, extends even to his relationships with others, even those closest to him, whom he sees but as means to a selfish end. There is no beauty in this.

Paradox (V)

Or else he, or she, loses himself in what is gaudy, in superficial show that has no truth, no authentic beauty, for it is void of love. St. Paul tells us that the beauty of a woman is not in pearls and braided hair and garments of gold. And so neither is there any beauty in the things man makes to display his great riches and the pride he takes in his power. How very empty of heart these things (and he) are.

Beauty is something profound and must be filled with love and truth and joy, not void of them. We are told that the beauty of a woman is found in her modesty and in her silent wisdom. But who can listen for this silence today amidst such noise? Who is there that treasures modesty? Humility, like obedience, is considered a curse, as man turns his back to God and presumes to create reality on his own. What ugliness such an attitude has wrought!

Far from radiating the beauty of the LORD evident in all Creation for those with eyes of purity, his mind is darkened, with his heart and his soul, and he finds relief from his burden only in death. But death will provide no peace, no beauty, for the soul that does not glorify God: he will remain blind even beyond the grave. If we do not seek the beauty of the hand of the LORD at work in this place – inclined rather to destroy what He has made – there will be nothing good for us to discover when this life is spent.

Seek the beauty of a kind and loving heart and you will find yourself surrounded by God's light.

13. Austerity

It is the feast of St. Benedict and my thoughts turn to the story (recounted in the Office for St. Scholastica) of his last yearly visit with his sister on the monastery grounds. The day had drawn to a close and it was time to end their spiritual conversation and return to their respective cells. But Scholastica begged her brother that they might pass the night together in continued prayer and dialogue.

He insisted not, that to break the rule thus was simply unacceptable (and perhaps scolded her for such a thought). She therefore turned to the LORD and pleaded for His intercession. Such a terrible thunderstorm ensued that none could move from where they sat all night. And so they passed the night together in prayerful conversation (though not before Benedict certainly did scold his sister for her action). A few days later Scholastica died and Benedict saw her soul flying to Heaven.

God listens to the sincere pleas of the humble of heart, and it must always be remembered that love trumps discipline, that every rule must bend to charity, since the greatest of all gifts is indeed love and God Himself is best revealed as love.

And so, important as our spiritual practices are, however necessary they may be to keep us on the path to the LORD and hasten our travel to Him, there is no practice that cannot be set aside when the greater call to love arises. Let us be faithful to the austerity that characterizes the narrow way, but most of all let our hearts always be open to the needs of others; for the LORD is concerned more for the care of His children than for the sacrifices we make. (He desires mercy, not sacrifice, after all.)

Paradox (V)

14. The Incarnation

The Word became flesh and so our faith, too, must become flesh, must become real as the flesh and blood of Jesus. Jesus is not an idea, some sort of abstract notion, but a man; God, of course, but also man: fully divine and fully human. And so our faith cannot remain an abstract idea, a maxim in a book, but must be *lived*, here, on this earth, with the flesh and blood that is ours.

God had to become man in order to save us, for in our fallen state we were unable to effect our own salvation. And the LORD couldn't just wave a magic wand to redeem our souls, for we are flesh and blood and possess a will (which has been compromised by our disobedience) – He could not take our will from us but had to acknowledge us as the creatures He made... and so He came among us as Man to save us. Thus does He recognize the importance of our flesh and blood (and sympathizes thoroughly with it), and thus does He leave our will free to accept or reject what is now in front of us: we can come to Him, embrace Him and follow Him on the way that clearly leads to life; or we can ignore or deny this great gift of His presence as light in our midst. (But know that He can do no more for us.)

Here is the great sign, the perfect revelation, of the Father's infinite love for us, here in the flesh of His Son (and in His crucifixion). Here He accepts to walk with the same dust that is upon our feet. We cannot say now that He is not real or that He does not care for us... for His humility destroys every such complaint. He is here, now, among us with His arms open toward us, answering every question of our souls. Take on His flesh and make real the faith you profess.

VI

1. Take Nothing

I know I have discussed the necessity of a spirit of poverty before, but it comes to me now the need of this spirit to permeate our lives day to day, that we must in a very real, tangible way be detached from the things at our hands... so that, even if we have many possessions we must deal with in our daily lives, none of them will we "take," none of them will we hold onto as our own but see them always as instruments to be used for the temporal needs of the passing day, again, that we might not pass with them but remain, even day to day, in the LORD's eternity.

We can remain undefiled by what we possess if indeed we keep our souls free from attachment to them, if we say always to ourselves that these are not our own, that they are ultimately of no worth... if we keep in mind and heart what matters most, which is, of course, the Kingdom of God (where no one possesses anything but all possess everything).

This is how it should be this day: to the best of our ability we should pray that all things will be "on earth as it is in Heaven," that somehow the LORD will infuse our souls with the spirit of poverty and we will readily employ all things for the common good – that possessing nothing we will possess everything, for His Kingdom will be ours.

This is practiced most particularly by our religious orders; but every man has a soul and must be the guardian and dispenser of the goods of his soul, constantly monitoring himself and determining if he is indeed *taking nothing* as he goes, or if he is like Lot's wife, who turned back with longing

Paradox (VI)

to look on what she owned and the life of sin she was called to leave behind... and so was turned to a pillar of salt. Our spirits should always readily flee to the hills.

2. He Suffers

We must take up our cross and walk with Christ; this is a command we cannot set aside. If He has suffered, we too must be willing to suffer – we must not stay away from joining Him on the wood. But, though we do certainly join ourselves to His pain, though we give our bodies over for crucifixion, it is always *He* who suffers, while our joining ourselves to Him sets us free from all trouble. (Thus it becomes a joy for us to suffer with Christ.)

I have experienced this on a few occasions (though not nearly as much as I should or as many others do). In the throes of some sickness or being put upon by some outside force whose instruments cause pain to the flesh, I have turned to Jesus and His Cross and sought to join Him there. And He has taken my place even as I take His place, and I have felt no pain, no suffering. My soul was at peace and my body at rest in His arms as I found myself ready to sacrifice my life, even to die, knowing a greater good would come.

My experiences are more likely to come in a dentist's chair than a torture chamber, more incidental than imposed by an oppressor, and so those Christians who are directly persecuted for their faith could speak with much more authority than I... but I think indication of how the Cross works in our lives can be gleaned even from such mundane trials.

Two Books

We all suffer in this life – there is no escaping our condition. So the question becomes what we do with our suffering, what we do with our lives. If we join our suffering with that of Jesus, true liberation from suffering will come. Failing this, I fear the suffering will overwhelm us weak mortal beings.

3. He Dies

Not only does Jesus suffer for us when we join Him on the Cross, when we walk in His way upon this earth, but He also dies for us (and most readily). And because He dies for us – in our stead – when we die with Him, utterly giving our lives into His hands unto the end, we do not die at all.

This is the only way for us to find eternal life, to be utterly preserved from death and live in the light of the LORD (who is Life) forever – that the Christ has died in our place. He has taken all our sins upon Himself, and so we suffer not for them; and He has loved us even unto death... and so we never die.

But we must indeed give our lives over to Him; we must indeed join Him in His death upon the Cross, not ashamed or afraid to trust all into His holy hands. Only then will we know the gift He holds for us in those pierced hands, in that pierced heart. (Apart from Him is only death for our bodies and our souls.)

"But what of Him?", you might ask, if you have compunction for the suffering and death He endures for your sake. What of His life? This you need not fear in the least, my child, for, though He has become man for us that He might die for our salvation, though He suffers unimaginably all the

Paradox (VI)

just punishment of mankind, and though He truly does die as man... He alone is able to rise again, even in His humanity, from the tomb to which our sins consign Him. For He is God and never dies in His divinity; and His divinity has the power to resurrect His body, even as it has our fallen humanity.

So do not turn away from such a gift, which has been offered for your sake. Do not make any excuse for not entering through the gates His wounds, His dying breath, have wrought by His grace. Die with Him and you shall live forever at His side.

4. Punishment

There must be punishment for our sins; for our own sakes, there must be punishment. So that the harmony and order of God's universe not be disturbed, there must be punishment to atone for our sin. In Himself God is not diminished at all by our sins, but we are diminished and Creation is diminished... and things must be set right, lest they grow only worse; and so punishment must be meted out. (We know this in our souls, I believe.)

If we do not align ourselves with the will of God, what can happen to us but that we be chastised? Removing ourselves from the righteous will of the almighty and ever living LORD brings chastisement upon us, I think one can say, immediately: for we thus separate ourselves from God, willfully, and this separation is itself a pain, a torture, to endure. But the punishment will hopefully bring us back in line with God's holy will, a will we can never overcome.

Yet there is something in this we cannot repay, a way in which whatever punishment we suffer is not enough – and so we have need of Jesus. If one is graced to be able to see just how greatly one's sins dishonor the LORD of Heaven and earth, if one is blessed to come to grips with just how (frighteningly) damaging the sin of the creature disobeying his Creator is – not to the Creator but to the creature – then one knows that any punishment inflicted upon us will fall infinitely short of recompense. (And this is not to mention we owe our LORD an overabundance.) It is only the Son who can truly express the sorrow we should have, only He who can bridge the chasm we have made and gain satisfaction, and forge reunion with our LORD.   Ultimately, only the punishment He undergoes is fruitful balm for the human soul.

5. Lost Souls

What will the LORD do about all the lost souls immersed in this culture of death? And what should the Church do? And so, what should we do?

There are so many who are so lost and the situation seems so desperate because no one seems to recognize their sin; no one admits their disobedience toward the commands of God and that which is written into our very beings. People think that what is wrong is right (and what is right is wrong) and so, what hope can there be that they will be cured of their blindness when it is so pervasive?

Jesus has taken the sins of all upon Himself and we must do the same. We must cry for the wounded hearts that turn away from the font of life to drink the polluted water of this forsaken place. Every day unwitting souls drink in the teaching of a corrupted world without seeming to give it a second thought. The tide is so strong and all that can stand

Paradox (VI)

against it is the sacrifice of Christ and our joining Him on the Cross: we must weep for those who go astray, praying with all our heart for their return.

There is much in ourselves that could be condemned, that leans in the direction of the wayward world, and so it is therefore easier for us to identify with the straying of those around us – and as for the strength needed to endure the pain, that comes alone from Jesus. But let us fear for souls, let us sympathize with their plight and think the best of them even as we remain firmly convinced that sin is sin. This conviction is what should bring us to tears even as we walk with them.

In the end we can but say, "Come, Lord Jesus." Come and wash clean an unholy world and let us wake as if from a dream to stand in your eternal light.

6. Found

It is Christ who finds us when we are lost, but first we must realize that we are lost and that only He has the power to find us. Otherwise we will be lost forever.

Only the lost can be found. Only that which is broken can be fixed. Only the dead can rise again. And so we repeat the basic truth all must embrace if they are to be Christians: we must die to ourselves to find our lives in Christ (which is the only life there is). Or we will be dead forever.

How lost we are! How in need of being found by the LORD and placed upon His shoulders to be carried home. We are so alone, so apart from the life that should be our own… so removed from the light of God. It is as if we have no form.

Two Books

In the beginning there was only darkness: the earth was void and without form – and we have sunk back into darkness and been tossed aside like a worthless ball. But a mass of useless flesh have we become.

And we have no idea of the way home, the way to the presence of the LORD, who brings order to our souls, to our lives. We sit in a strange land with no map, no directions, no sense of where we are or where we are going – thus we shall ever be until we trust in Jesus. He is our compass, our way, for only He is Truth and holds all truth and would impart all truth, the truth that redeems us.

Again, the final test is death. Do we have the faith that the LORD can save us even from what seems our absolute end, that He has the power to raise us from the grave to walk with Him in freedom? It is He who finds us when we are lost; only He has the power. This is the lesson we must learn, the faith we must employ.

7. Malleable

How malleable we are when we are dead! We may be moved this way or that, offering no resistance. It is thus we must put ourselves in the Hand of God, and so be as clay in the hands of the Potter.

If we are not dead, how resistant our wills are to the movement of the Spirit upon us, especially if such movement does not please our flesh. Thus, how inclined we are to complain!

But those who are deeply set in Christ do not resist whatever may come, for all – even the worst of circumstances – is taken in His Name. For why should we resist the will of

Paradox (VI)

Him who loves us most (even more than we ourselves) and knows better than any what is best for us and what will satisfy us most deeply?

And so, let us be dead, let us be malleable as clay, giving way to the imprint of His seal – let us indeed be sealed indelibly and willingly by the Holy Spirit and never rebel against His working in our lives. Let us rather celebrate all that comes to us by His Hand, realizing that all that comes to us is indeed by His Hand. Then we shall be truly happy, as we were meant to be. Then the LORD's will shall be fulfilled in us, and we will dwell with Him eternally.

Eternity begins now even as death begins now – it is our call every day. We need not wait to die to the world, nor to be reborn in Christ and live our new life. It is upon us now: Jesus is the Resurrection and the Life. And so, let us die this day, offering ourselves entirely into the Hand of God that He might form us as He pleases. Why should we wait or hesitate or hold anything back from Him? By this time we should be aware of the great blessings that come from faith, and desire those blessings to be fulfilled. Let us be moved by the LORD this day!

8. The Weight of Glory

St. Paul speaks of the weight of glory we shall know in the eternal presence of our LORD, blessed by Him forever – in the light of His face we will praise His NAME! And he speaks of the light burden we bear as we make our way through this world to the beatific vision, carrying our cross all the while.

We know that the burden Paul bore was anything but light according to the standards of this world – again, he made that abundantly clear for us in recounting (against his will) all the sufferings he endured for the sake of the Gospel: the beatings and stonings, imprisonments and shipwrecks, sleepless nights and snakebites, as well as the constant anxiety for his children… and in the end his beheading. So if his burden was not light by worldly standards, it must have been light by some other measure, or perhaps just in comparison to the weight of glory to which he strove.

The weight upon him could have been light because, as we have indicated elsewhere, it is Jesus who carries our cross for us, assuming the brunt of the burden; but let us consider now more closely indeed how light is any burden we bear on earth when cast in the light of eternal glory. What would one not endure to acquire such blessing? With this crown in mind, what matters any persecution? Indeed, the persecutions may thus be turned to joy!

How heavy is that weight of glory! How all-encompassing is God's love. Our LORD is as a Giant and we but ants, and so is His glory in relation to our sacrifices.

Let us set our hearts and minds on that glory; let us strive toward it with all our strength. Then our souls will be free from all disturbance – then our spirits will readily rise to Heaven.

9. The Weight of Misery

O LORD, how do we escape the weight of misery this world brings upon us and we bring upon ourselves by our sin? How can we be saved from the snares of the devil and find ourselves in the freedom of your presence? How shall

Paradox (VI)

we be made a new creation and walk with your Son in holiness and truth, and so fear nothing of this world or Satan?

Please lift this weight of misery from us! Please set us free from the weakness of the flesh. Let your Spirit fall upon us that we might be born again.

Of course, the weight of misery has been taken from us by the mercy of Christ and His sacrifice. Of course, we have nothing left to fear and no reason to doubt the glory that comes to us thereby… yet we live our lives in earthen vessels and so remain prone to the temptations of the devil wrought by the glamour of this passing world. And so the question is more so: when will our joy become complete? When shall the weight of misery be lifted from us forever?

The weight of misery has indeed been wrought into our flesh by the sin of Adam and our own participation therein. Thus does Paul wish to be away from the body and in the presence of the LORD in Heaven – thus does he wish for his salvation to be complete. But he is willing to remain for the sake of others (all in accord with the Father's will). He sees purpose in enduring the Cross further, knowing that such service in the Name of Jesus will bring good fruits to others.

Such should be our attitude – though certainly we yearn for the Day when we will live in the eternal light of the Kingdom, our hearts should be set on service of others, as the Lord demands and as He has shown us. And in this blessed service of others, in this freely giving of our lives for the salvation of souls, the weight of misery may be lifted from them, and further lifted from us as well, as we are drawn closer to God's presence.

10. Forgetfulness

How forgetful we can be of the grace God has given us, of the blessings we have known by His Spirit and in His sacraments... and indeed in our very lives. How often we forget to thank Him and praise Him for His glory and His goodness to us. And how forgetful we can be with others, failing to share that grace given us, to be the image of Christ in this world. It is a shame.

We cannot forget the grace of God at work in our lives or neglect to share it with others; this is a forgetfulness to be avoided, to be repented. But there is a forgetfulness to be desired, of which our mystic saints often speak – a forgetfulness not of God, but of the things of this earth.

As we have previously said, one great saint calls this the cloud of forgetting, which we must enter if we are to discover God. St. John of the Cross speaks of the dark night of the senses and the dark night of the spirit, which serve to purge us of all that is not of the LORD in our bodies and in our souls; and, again, this forgetfulness, this abandonment of earthly attachments, must be endured if our LORD is to become known to us.

Some saints have spoken of being unable to function well at their tasks, their practical responsibilities, for days and even months at a time, so taken from themselves do they become by the grace of God (a grace that should never be forgotten). But one must be clear in discerning such a rare blessing from mere irresponsibility or indeed forgetfulness of the things of God.

Let us forget ourselves and every concern for our lives and give all to God – this is the challenge for every Christian. Let us place ourselves in His hands and allow Him to carry us through our days (unto Heaven).

11. Remembrance

And how important is remembrance! If we forget the LORD we are lost, and so we must remember Him always. He has called us to remember His NAME, His presence among us in the divine Silence; and we are called also to remember the sacrifice He has made for our sins. "Do this in remembrance of me," the Son says at the institution of the Eucharist, at the hour of His death. God is with us in His NAME and in the Body and Blood we receive at His altar.

But remembering is more than simply keeping in mind, though it may begin there. We must become as members of His Body, one with Him – this is true re-membrance of Him; this is the fulfillment of His call. In the holy sacrifice of the Mass, the offering He has made becomes present to us (in a bloodless fashion) and we are again at the foot of the Cross, at the table of the first Eucharist. And receiving His Body and Blood truly present to us, we truly become filled with His presence – the presence we know spiritually in His NAME – and so become united with Him, and so become as members of His Body.

His arms and legs we are, His eyes and ears and heart. This is true remembrance, indeed. Filled with His Spirit we become flesh of His flesh and bone of His bone, His light shining in our eyes.

O let us be children of that holy light, surrounded by the Spirit of Christ and walking in His footsteps! Let us never set aside His Cross or close our hearts to His call. We must be as

Jesus living now in this world.... This is the role of His Church.

Let us do all in remembrance of our LORD. (Then we shall be blessed.)

12. Free Will

I've gotten rather far along in this work and do not recall if I have treated the subject of free will directly... but I will approach it now.

Freedom exists only in God, who is absolutely free and wills what He wills. His will is unchanging and He is immutable, but He is subject to no necessity; for indeed all comes to be only by His will, and so nothing precedes His will or impinges upon it, except what He wills. This freedom is magnificent and awe-inspiring, and indeed covers Creation as water covers the sea.

And we may participate in this freedom with Him. Thus has He made us in His image. He calls us to join Him in His freedom and gives us a share in His free will that we might choose such glory, that such freedom might be known even by His poor creatures. But, again, it is only in Him that freedom is found.

People do as they please and call it freedom without recognizing the slavery they take upon themselves, for it makes them indebted to so many things (things to which true freedom is not subject). And so by their actions contrary to the freedom found in God – essentially, in their sin – they find themselves beset by any number of diseases that are bred in such separation from the LORD and His will. They become subject to fear, subject to hatred, subject to lust and greed and pride and many other evils that debilitate the soul and bring it into slavery under the devil's sway. But to them the devil is a fantasy, and so their slavery to him becomes complete: no freedom is left for them to overcome that which they deny... and so they become less than human, having lost the light of the LORD our God.

Let us not dwell overmuch on the slavery of others but rejoice in the tremendous freedom found in God, which indeed covers the earth like the light of the sun – though this Sun never sets and is never obstructed by anything at all. True freedom is absolute surrender to the will of God. Alleluia!

13. Predestination

How great is our God, in whom complete freedom is joined with complete knowledge of all that is, all that was, and all that shall ever be; who sees all in a single glance... from whose heart all good things come.

Freedom and predestination are not contradictory in the omniscient love of the LORD, who sees all and is in all and through whom all comes to be. He is free to act and He is free to know – nothing escapes His power or His wisdom, for all is held in His Hand and in His Mind.

And so He sees what shall be, for, though to us the future seems a distant thing, for Him it has already been. A man can only become dizzy contemplating the glorious splendor and knowledge of God, but He is in no way made unsteady or unsure. This steadfastness He would share with us all, and those who give themselves (like children) entirely to His free will begin to glimpse the awesome specter of the eternity that exists as a single moment.... But while this flesh is upon us, who can stand but a fleeting vision of the vast wonder of our LORD?

All is determined by the LORD in His absolute freedom. From beginning to end all is known by Him and all is drawn by His holy Hand. Yet freedom He has planted in the heart of every man to choose whether he will go along with His blessed plan or harden his heart against it. The LORD already knows the answer yet the freedom still abides... and is itself what can condemn a man.

Only in praise and rejoicing do we come to understand the glorious harmony of the LORD's divine plan and how freedom and predestination can be one and the same. For only in rejoicing do we come to know Him. Sing Alleluia to the light of God!

14. Love

It is love that accounts for the expansive reach of our LORD, for His freedom and His omniscience, His being everywhere at all times and seeing and knowing all things. All of this is because He loves, because He is love.

No walls stand in the way of love, of His unconditional, absolute love of all. The fact that He loves all (the fact that He loves) accounts for the fact that He understands all things. It is only by love that we understand anything, and He who is all love thus understands all things.

We must enter into that love, that all-encompassing, all-embracing love of God; only then will we begin to know and understand Him who is love... only by beginning to know and understand as He does. His love shines on the evil and

Paradox (VI)

the good, it is obstructed by nothing, and so all obstructions to love we must remove from our hearts.

In the end, John, the beloved apostle, the great Evangelist, has the most profound word, the most profound sense of the LORD: *God is love*. There is nothing to be said after this and nothing that can be said better reveals the nature of God. His silent NAME, the divine Word – YHWH – brings us into His presence (where there is only love), but as for human expression, as for words that find audible pronunciation – none characterizes our LORD better than love.

May this word be saved from all the ravages it undergoes by sinful man set upon following his own plans, and so defining the word as he pleases. We are not God and so we do not know love except as He reveals it to us. Let us follow His command to love in the way He leads and we will not fall short of the glory of the LORD.

VII

1. Empty Me of Myself

I cannot emphasize enough the importance of emptying ourselves of ourselves, of the fat of sin and selfishness that so weighs us down in this life. The LORD must enter our souls, must come to make His home in us, and this cannot occur as long as we are full of ourselves, of our own desires and wants, led by our own will. (This is but the path to destruction.)

And so, in prayer we must lay down our arms, lay down our bodies and our minds, give our will to Him who made us and wishes to save us... and perhaps come to tears, crying out to Him in our emptiness. He will listen.

The LORD always listens to us; He always hears us, and especially our cries. We need but make a motion in His direction, but say the words "Help me, LORD!" and we will find the help we need. But we must seek it: we must open our mouths. (Do not suffocate as you are, my brother.)

If we are willing to lay down our lives, to empty ourselves of ourselves, being thus purged by the touch of His hand – under which we tremble – then we shall find the LORD; then He will approach us to make His home in us. And then we will know emptiness and fear no more.

How oppressive it is to become full of oneself, to be filled with anxiety and short of breath. How desperately we need to set aside all our ills, all the disease that afflicts our soul, and come to Him.

O LORD, thank you for being before me this day, leading me to your Kingdom.

Paradox (VII)

2. To Die Is To Live

Certainly we have seen this in Christ and that it must be so in the life of every Christian (and is ultimately true in Jesus' death and resurrection), but today I think especially of the role of a man, especially a husband and a father, whose call is to lay down his life, to die, for his wife and children (much as St. Paul describes for us in Ephesians 5).

The woman is to live, it seems to me; she too is called to sacrifice, but to bring life, while the man is to die... indeed, much as the Church is to live and Jesus is to die for His Bride. This is how love works, both in the theological and ultimate sense, and in day to day life. The woman is to live and the man is to die.

This is perhaps most obviously seen in the man's readiness to go to war, literally to die to protect others, most especially women and children. This is his glory, his happiness, his call. And it is only natural he do so when it is necessary (though we pray it ought never be necessary and that all may live in love, in peace...).

It is also evident in man's work, his daily labor to support his wife and children. There is certainly a dying here, a suffering the man must willingly undergo. A man cannot think of himself, of his own wants and desires, or chaos will ensue, and he himself will die on the day he does so. He must work for others.

We see this too, of course, in the sacrifice the martyrs make for the faith. They do not think of themselves but only of their duty toward God, and so toward His Church. (It is from their blood the Church grows.)

And so the man must die to live, and indeed lives to die. This is his blessed call and purpose in life, which has been made so clear in Christ.

3. Work

Man must work. There is no denying this. But how does one define work and accomplish it rightly? It may be simply stated as doing the will of God, but let us look more closely at the question.

In twenty-first century America, work is generally equated with making money. Many see work as something done against one's will, a painful trial. Work may also be defined more positively as employing one's talent, or as something performed for the benefit of others. I think in all these definitions there is validity and necessity… but one must be clear about just what one means.

Certainly in a Christian context the employment of one's God-given talent is of utmost importance, for each of us is called by the LORD to some work in this world – and burying our talent in the ground tempts the fires of Gehenna. And that our vocation should benefit others could not be more obvious, considering Christ's essential call to serve.

But the other definitions are not without merit. Money cannot be the leading purpose of one's work, lest one lose one's soul in pursuit of the world, but we know we must accept the responsibility of supporting ourselves and our dependents, for as St. Paul has stated: those unwilling to work should not eat. Thus there is a practical necessity to work. And as for suffering, does Jesus not call us to take up our cross daily? But one should be careful that the suffering that

Paradox (VII)

comes with work is redemptive, is indeed in union with the Lord and His Cross, and not something that debilitates the body as immoderate pursuit of money debilitates the soul. Good fruit should always be borne.

It is not easy to discern one's vocation and hear clearly the way the LORD calls... and just how much emphasis to put on each definition will vary according to one's particular state in life – but let us continually seek to discern our call, asking ourselves if we are truly doing the will of God.

4. The Mustard Seed

If we are to have faith the size of a mustard seed, it is not that our faith (or the apostles') needs to be bigger.... In fact, it needs to be smaller. We must be humble as the mustard seed or we are without faith.

One could say further that faith has no size: if we have faith, we have faith; if we don't, we don't. We put our trust in the LORD or we are lost – there is nothing else. But that faith, if we have it, is by nature humble, is by nature childlike... is by nature very small. Really, it is as a breath, the Breath of God upon our souls, and nothing more.

It is in small things the LORD makes His home, not in the rich and powerful of this world. These He does not know; these do not know Him at all. The LORD indeed uses the weak to shame the strong, and there is nothing smaller than a mustard seed. And so, to the size of this seed we are called.

The Spirit is invisible, God is immaterial (more humble than a speck of dust, if you will). And we must be like Him; we must approach His transcendence, His separation from the things of this world. It is true that God has become Man to lead us to the Kingdom – but the Kingdom itself is beyond this world, though in its midst it may be.

How shall we be like the mustard seed, we who are so attached to what we see, who are so intent on growing according to the ways of this world? How shall we be set free to walk the plane of Heaven? Let us be like Jesus, who could walk on water; let there be no weight upon us to cause us to sink into the deep. O LORD, help us to be free! Let us grow unto Thee.

5. Perfection

Jesus calls the young man to perfection. He looks upon him with love and invites him to sell all he owns and follow Him. He calls him close to Himself, to walk along with Him, where there are no worldly cares, where all is cared for by the LORD.

I have noted in another work that in first instructing the young man to keep the commandments, Jesus mentions only those referring to love of neighbor – the first three, concerning love of God, are omitted. And certainly by inviting the man to sell all and give it to the poor, and follow Him, Jesus is focusing now on love of God, on realizing how good the LORD is and giving all to Him.

But I notice now that Jesus also omits the commands regarding covetousness, both of our neighbor's goods and his wife. Is it because this is the young man's particular sin, evident in his attachment to his worldly possessions, in his great sadness at the prospect of losing them? Is it only the perfect call to Christ that will heal him of this sin?

Paradox (VII)

It is a question for us all: What keeps us from the perfection of the LORD, and how does He call us to such perfection? Do we all need to sell all we own? Such an action, such commitment, such trust in God should be of assistance to any soul… but can the same faith and trust be shown, can perfection be as fully achieved, while *not* selling all one owns and giving it to the poor?

It is the following of the LORD that matters, that is *everyone's* call – we all must be perfect as He. We must have complete faith in Him, we must be ready to give up all for Him, to lay down our lives in His Name… but as for the way in which we follow Him up the road, the manner in which we embrace His call and achieve perfection – the particular call may be different for each soul. But all must thirst as the young man for eternal life, for perfection, and obey the LORD's instructions when He draws us into His arms.

Take my life, O LORD; take all I own (even my very breath).

6. Fear

Fear of the LORD is the beginning of wisdom; without it we will know nothing, we will remain ignorant and blind. For if we do not know the LORD, who is Creator of all that is, then we can know nothing of what is. And to know the LORD is nothing if not a fearful thing (for, again, He is Creator of all that is).

How can we small creatures stand before the LORD of all? And yet, if we do not come into His presence, if we do not know Him, our lives are utterly vain.

And so we must not be afraid to experience the fear of the LORD. We cannot in false humility refuse to approach Him. This would be vanity as well – we would remain ever empty. And this is not His will.

And so, when the Word of God exhorts us repeatedly not to be afraid, not to give in to fear, it means not only fear for our lives or fear about the things of the world (which are as nothing), but also that we should not avoid coming to the LORD because of the fear that will inevitably come upon us as His light begins to encompass us.

It is indeed a fearful thing to stand before God; we should never presume it to be a facile act, never take it casually, as if it were a small matter. We should rather overcome the fear by coming as children before Him, with utter trust in our hearts, and the reverent fear every child should have for his father. This fear, born of truth and love, will sustain us. And He will quickly place His arms around us and surround us with His love.

7. The Body of Christ

How closely united we should be with Jesus! We must be as His Body, He as our Head. Our breath should be His breath, our heart His heart. Every move we make, every step we take, should be done in Him. O how far short we fall of our call!

The Body is one, Scripture says, and we should work together as one Body in Christ. A harmonious whole the Church should be, must be, reflecting the mind of Christ, inspired by His Spirit. But how fragmented the Body is!

Paradox (VII)

One in Him, one with one another, living and breathing with our Lord and aiding each other in our walk with Him... this is the way we are called. Yet there is much work left to be done; many wounds need to be healed within us and among us.

Only Jesus can bring us healing, only He can make us one – and only we can decide to follow His call. There is hope; there is always hope. Jesus stands at the door knocking still.... Will we let Him in?

Does Jesus speak in you, my brother? Are you His hands and feet? Do you live for Him alone? He wants to live and breathe in you, to work through you – are you a Christian in deed?

The Body is one and has many members and all its members are of the Lord. Let Him look through your eyes. Let Him speak through your mouth. Let Him walk with your feet and touch with your hands. Let Him live in this world in His Body: let us be the Body of Christ.

8. Virgin Mother

And a virgin shall conceive and bear a son. And a Virgin has conceived and borne a Son. And she remains both Virgin and Mother for all eternity, continually maintaining her purity while continually bearing fruit, on this earth and in Heaven. For she is Mother not only of Jesus but also His Church; and as immaculately as she was conceived, so immaculate does she stay (especially now in the Presence of God).

How can a woman be both virgin and mother; how can a bush aflame not be consumed? How can God, who is beyond our comprehension, come to dwell with man? The LORD is much greater than we and can do all things, and does all things that are good, that are beneficial to our souls. Thus has He made Mary both Virgin and Mother; thus Jesus is born in our midst… thus all souls are called into His Kingdom.

How glorious is the Queen arrayed in gold who stands beside Christ on His throne, who is ever at His side, ever united with Him and doing His will, dispensing His graces upon us. She is not God but is in union with Him, as all Christians are called to be.

How can we be partakers of divine nature? Would we not burn to ash upon approaching His fire? How can a member of the corrupted human race come to be with the LORD? All these things of which we speak are impossible, except by the will of God (who holds all things in His hands).

And so, that a woman could be both virgin and mother should not astonish us – it should instill in our souls great hope.

9. Compassion

There may be no more misused word than compassion, which is more often than not misguided and become its opposite. Those in favor of euthanasia employ it freely; those promoting abortion cling to it… in so many ways society has its heart inverted when it comes to the meaning of compassion.

Compassion means to suffer with, not to eliminate suffering; for eliminating suffering is impossible, and attempts to do so invariably end up only increasing suffering for all involved.

Paradox (VII)

Women find themselves in problematic pregnancies and are told the solution is to abort the child. The answer is not to take their hand and be at their side throughout their trials; the answer is not compassion, but rather to take the so-called easy way out. But unless a woman has a heart of stone, she is only bringing a suffering upon herself that will last a lifetime... and, of course, a baby is dead (and so many souls are corrupted by their involvement).

A man is old or depressed or terminally ill, and instead of society respecting and supporting their elderly and sick, it seeks to eliminate them (not their suffering) from the scene. A person is told he is going to die, and so he thinks to kill himself – why wait for the inevitable? There is no sense that these last days, these difficult years, could be a blessing for both the suffering soul and those who care for him. There is no sense of true compassion at all, nor that there is something beyond this material world. His is but a useless life.

But where do these easy, "compassionate" paths lead but a culture and a society without love, without compassion. (And those whose hearts still beat are viewed as obstacles to a brave new world.)

10. Maturity

It is much the purpose of this writing to address maturity, to assist souls in finding maturity in the faith, that they might no more be like children, like leaves blown here and there, not knowing where they are going. There is great difficulty in discerning the truth in a society so corrupted by lies, by half-truths... by sin. And so I must encourage everyone to think carefully about what they believe and why – in essence, to be steeped in the teaching of the Church.

Let the saints be our guide in seeking maturity in faith, since they have discovered it now in Heaven (since they pursued it so diligently while on earth). In the end we simply give ourselves to the will of God; on the way we need only follow the directions of our Mother (Mary and the Church) – these foundations set firmly in place, we cannot but grow to maturity each day.

Essentially, though, a mature person is a selfless person, one who thinks of God and others before himself. We come back always to the service and sacrifice of Christ, which is the keynote of this work, and, overall, to being as children (as He has told us we must be).

But how can it be that first I say we must be as children no more, and then that in the end it is children we must be? Is this not contradictory? It should not be difficult to discern. The child we must abandon is the one subject to the whispers and wiles of this corrupted world, a soul unable to distinguish right from wrong, and so, often falling into wrong. (This child one can be at any age.) The child we must become is a son of God, our eyes fixed on Him alone.

(And when we are mature, the sickle is put to the root… and we are swept into His arms.)

11. Broken Cisterns

Man has abandoned God and made for himself broken cisterns which hold no water. And so he is dying of thirst.

Only the Word of God, only the LORD Himself, can quench our thirst; only He can satisfy our deepest longing,

Paradox (VII)

our most pressing needs. But we turn away from Him, sometimes blithely, sometimes boldly, and so cut ourselves off from His nourishment, from His grace. And instead we drink from polluted waters.

All we have left is the mud beneath our feet, and that offers sore consolation. All we have is what our hands have made, and how soon these things fall apart (more quickly than we ourselves). How empty are our lives.

But who can see this? Who can see that we drink from broken cisterns? And who will turn from such futility?

The end is on the horizon; it is not far away. It draws closer every day.... There is little time left to be saved. Do not waste the day.

As the broken cisterns multiply, as they fill the earth and draw souls astray, what hope have we of preserving our lives if we do not quickly turn back to the LORD, to His Word?

His Word is all that will nourish us; His Word is all that Is. Do not embrace the emptiness but take up the cup of blessing and live.

12. Healing Wounds

Only the LORD heals even as He wounds; only His chastisement is life-giving. We may, if we are blessed, imitate His ways... but it is always He who heals (even as He wounds).

The LORD does everything out of love, and so whatever punishment we may suffer at His hands is only for our benefit, only motivated by His concern for our immortal souls. He has made us and He desires us to share in His love, and so He does what He can to lead us there. Though it may be difficult for us to endure at times, the pain is indeed sweet to the Christian soul.

When we think of wounds, we think of that which harms us, which diminishes us somehow. Wounds make us less able to live our lives as we should; they impair us and often leave us afraid and alone.... They are things to be avoided, and mourned when they come.

And there may be a certain mourning in the wounds God inflicts; a certain sadness may come to our souls. But if we set our hearts upon His will, if we truly desire to be Christian, we will know all the while that the wounds He imparts are a blessing, a particularly great blessing for our spiritual lives.

They are certainly a sharing in the wounds of Christ, which serve to redeem the world; but their grace is more intimate still – though becoming united with the sacrifice of Jesus is an honor and a glory most to be esteemed, the wounds we receive at the hand of our LORD touch us very personally as well, serving to fulfill our deepest needs and indeed healing us of our afflictions.

How can afflictions remedy afflictions; how can wounds heal? Perhaps it is that the touch of God is one that cannot but heal, that cannot but draw us into His love.

13. Bright Cloud

At the Transfiguration a bright cloud overshadowed the three apostles, and they became fearful. A shining darkness enveloped them and almost overwhelmed them. The Father's presence shook them to the marrow, too much to bear... but Jesus reached down and touched them, and assured them He was there.

Paradox (VII)

How can a cloud be bright; how can darkness shine? How can He who is the Light of all be covered by and reveal Himself in a dark cloud? How else could He reveal Himself?

How overwhelming is the presence of God to the mortal mind, to our poor souls! How it must frighten us (or we are fools). We cannot stand in the presence of God, in the Light of His all-consuming fire, and so in His mercy He comes to us shadowed by a cloud. (Else we would indeed die of fear.)

But His brightness cannot be hidden, cannot be extinguished – for even darkness is not dark to Him but possesses the brightest of light. And so the cloud that surrounds Him, that shields Him from our eyes (that we might not look directly into this blinding Sun), cannot but be bright, cannot but shine... or He would not be in the cloud at all.

Jesus is like the bright cloud: He is God, He is light... yet He is robed in flesh for our sakes, that we might look upon Him, that we might gaze upon God and not die.

O LORD, may our eyes adjust to the Light that surpasses all our understanding, that overwhelms our minds, that we might stand with your Son in your presence and praise you for your grace and mercy.

14. The Day and the Hour

No one knows the day and the hour of Jesus' return. Though false prophets abound in this regard, it is not for us to know – it is for us to expect Him. For He may come at any moment; at every moment He stands at the door. He is always near.

Today is the day of salvation, now *is* the acceptable time. Approach Him and you will know His presence beating in your heart. Live as children of light awaiting His glory, longing for His return, and you will have Him near you indeed.

That Day is much avoided by the sinner, who takes his refuge in darkness; but he shall soon be exposed to the light and have nowhere left to hide. How the sinner fears His coming! How he cries out like the demons: "You have come to destroy us!" For he knows his evil cannot stand in the light of God.

But we who are children of that light should welcome His coming, should indeed long for that Day… should, as we have said, hold it in our hearts and treasure it above all else, calling out with all the Church: "Come, Lord Jesus!" For the Spirit and the Bride say "Come" and all who love the LORD cannot but wish His presence among us, finally, and completely.

You should thirst for that coming Day and Hour, my brother. You should taste it in your mouth like the blood of Christ you raise to your lips and profess with them:

> The Kingdom of Heaven is at hand.
> Repent and believe in the Gospel.

2

Hippie Convert

Hippie Convert

There once was a hippie named James
who wore patches all over his jeans,
for he wanted very much
to be like Neil Young
on the cover of *After the Gold Rush*.

It's true he was too young
to slog through the mud at Woodstock –
being only nine at the time –
but when he became a teen,
this icon stole his imagination.

And so, though slightly out of time,
his heart still beat
and he was no less obsessed
with long hair and marijuana,
not to mention LSD.

Peace and love meant everything to him –
Jesus spoke of this, did He not? –
and the bandana-ed souls with flowers everywhere
proclaimed these words constantly…
So why not join their ranks?

Of course, there was also John Lennon –
who could be cooler than him?
He was always imagining peace
and speaking truth to power…
it was easy to get lost in his dream.

Every adolescent
wants to impress his friends
and will often go along to be 'in',
and so James traveled many wayward paths
that led inevitably to sin.

The foolishness of youth
accounts for much
of the blindness in our eyes,
but everyone is responsible in the end
for his soul's condition.

But how can the blind recognize their call
while living in a pipe dream?
How can the unreality of our lives
be seen when it is so veiled?
And so, how can we be redeemed?

It is a certain slavery
into which we fall
when led by something other than the LORD,
when love becomes confused…
and peace completely false.

From the beginning the devil is a liar;
in his heart he ever conceives
deceptions that cause
the unwise to be misguided,
to lose all sense and clarity.

We are not even aware as it happens,
especially when we are young,
for the culture is pervaded
by a preponderance of pollution
that entices our hearts and minds.

And so, though James was raised
in a Catholic home
and educated in Catholic schools,
his soul was not safe from the influence of Satan –
even these were infiltrated by evil.

I.

1. What Is a Hippie?

What is this creature
the culture has concocted
and put forth as a "hippie"?
I am not a historian,
but will offer a few observations.

It blossomed in the 60's
but was spawned before that
in the hipsters of earlier decades.
I suppose it may have its origins
in the class known as "gypsies."

But, again, I am no historian
and this is not my concern;
my story is much more personal,
an autobiography of sorts,
not a case study.

And so I will speak
of what hippies are to me
and the way in which I have been one…
and perhaps still hold some of their qualities
even after my conversion.

Two Books

On the positive side,
hippies are childlike, are they not?
Dealing in ideals as they do
and believing all things
spoken to them…

There is a certain innocence there,
and even a sense of wonder.
But one wonders how much of this
is produced by the haze of drugs
and how much is sincere.

Thus we have leaned in to the negative side:
how real is the peace and love
the hippie proclaims,
and how faithfully does he follow it
in all its travails?

Ahhh, travails! What of suffering?
Here is perhaps the key of my conversion:
the truth is not known or professed
without a willingness to sacrifice –
and this the childish hippie lacks.

Hippie Convert (I)

Jesus has called us to be like children –
we cannot enter Heaven if we are not.
And so innocence and humility
are much to be treasured…
Then where does childishness enter in?

Differentiating the childish
from the childlike
is perhaps the heart of our task:
for when selfishness takes over,
the child loses his savor.

The hippie tends to think of himself,
and so can fall into judgment of others.
He is often able to forgive sins
that are like his own,
but those different he readily condemns.

This is childish
and shows a lack of vision,
a worldview void of understanding –
in him all wisdom is gone,
for his heart is set on his own pleasure.

A preoccupation with pleasure
is the downfall of the flower child,
the pleasure of drugs, the pleasure of sex,
and all the sensual delights
the world offers.

The LORD has made us
to delight in His Creation,
to find joy in the life He has given us;
but the brokenness of man
requires such impulse to be tempered.

If he were not fallen,
man would not be inclined
to inordinate pleasures…
and all would be well.
There would be no need for restraint.

But since his godly form is distorted,
he desires what he should not,
and so must learn to control himself.
But the hippie loses all sense of proportion
and gives himself over to every desire.

Hippie Convert (I)

This seems wise in his eyes
because he does not recognize
his brokenness.
All seems well, and even blessed…
and so, blindly he rambles along.

His head is in the sky
and it seems he does fly
with great ease through his days.
Perhaps it is his innocence
that makes him unable to see.

But innocence itself must be tempered
by wisdom, as our Lord has said,
or innocence will be only ignorance
and cause man to sin,
to embrace something quite unlike innocence.

We cannot sin and claim innocence,
for this is utter foolishness –
innocence and sin are opposed
and cannot be drawn together,
except by the ignorant soul.

Two Books

The hippie is a kind of fool,
evoking pity perhaps,
often meaning well,
but sinning nonetheless
against himself and others.

One can claim naiveté
but the results are just the same:
taking drugs and fornicating
do not engender peace and love,
only the very opposite.

Is one unfamiliar with the drug trade
and all the violence it brings?
Does the hippie think he is not a part of this?
And is he unaware, too, of the violence
in the poisoning of his soul?

And does one think nothing
of broken hearts and cut skin,
or of aborted children?
There is no scent of flowers here
in this empty love.

2. What of This Empty Love?

There is more to be said
of the hippie's redeeming qualities,
for there is some sense of peace of love
that may become fruitful
if united with the Cross of Christ.

But it is the dark side
that beckons to be told
as I sit here this morning
in the presence of the Lord.
I must speak more of the empty love.

This love does not seem empty
to the blinded soul,
and indeed some genuineness may be there
in his thirst for pleasure…
but it is pleasure he seeks.

It leads him to ignore the ways
in which the other becomes an object,
an instrument of pleasure
like any other modern tool –
why not just love the one you're with?

Two Books

One wonders where their hearts are.
Are they on the other,
or are they preoccupied with themselves,
with no sense of sacrifice
or, dare I say, commitment?

How this commitment is lacking
where bodies become things
to be used and cast off
when they prove useful no more –
where is love in this?

I remember in college
a talented artist made a drawing
of a man with a void for a heart.
I was attracted to it, I knew not why,
though later I realized it was a portrait of me.

O the emptiness
that fills the soul
so blinded by his pride and lust!
Will he wake one day
and recognize his vanity?

Hippie Convert (I)

How confident he is
that he sees and knows,
that he really cares about others;
how well he is able
to fool himself.

This is the remarkable thing:
they think themselves most compassionate
who most disregard
the dignity of others
and care not even for themselves.

How will they find the humility
not to trust in their own will,
to understand the ways in which
they remain so sinful?
Every mature soul must come to this.

There is a seriousness that is missing,
a failure to recognize that this is not a child's game,
that we hold our lives in our hands
and can severely damage them,
and others in our realm.

Two Books

Are we kings who rule as we please?
Are we led by our eyes
like Lot to the land of Sodom?
We who seem so carefree,
do we care to know where we are going?

It is to a strange town we are misguided,
a place we'd never expected to be,
a place inimical to our souls
where sickness reigns,
where we are plagued by disease.

There we cannot control our hands
for they have a mind of their own,
trained as they have been
by the free rein given them
by what has become a lifeless spirit.

This emptiness, this vanity of vanities,
this hell on earth
is the fate
of those led alone by pleasure –
they find themselves in a barren wasteland.

3. The Wasteland

So barren is the wasteland of this world,
so empty of life;
how the word of the Lord has proven true:
we call blessed
those who never bore children.

How Rachel weeps
for the millions heaped
in piles upon the altars
of a society obsessed with lust
and defensive of its own convenience.

It is hard not to see the hippie's role
in this carnage.
Innocently enough he began
preaching against war and anything
that smacked of violence.

But here is where his free love leads,
to the greatest violence known to man:
the slaughter of his own children in the womb
and the self-assured grin
reserved for those who question him.

Contraception seems a facile solution,
a simple means to keep children
from getting in the way
of one's unbounded pleasure,
and of course to limit the race.

Sterility is indeed the ideal
of the soul enclosed in his ego,
of him for whom convenience is king;
and anything that prevents such freedom
is simply a bothersome thing.

And so, let there be no offspring,
no one to care for but ourselves.
Would this not be paradise?
Is this not the goal of our race?
All evidence points in this direction.

Contraception completes the movement
toward making the body an object
to be manipulated to one's advantage,
according to our carnal desires.
And what is there more than this?

Hippie Convert (I)

Nothing. What else could there be?
What else do we need
but freedom to do as we please?
And contraception facilitates this, does it not?
And it keeps the blood from rising up.

Yet the blood rises more and more;
the death such selfishness deals
cannot be undone
by selfishness itself –
should this not be obvious?

The lust is hereby increased;
the blood now boils in the veins…
and the pale mask of contraception
is soon exposed for its failure
to prevent what is dreaded most.

And so the baby must be killed –
we never wanted such a thing anyway.
And by all means this must be done
or we shall not be able to go on.
And so the need for sterility becomes clear.

Two Books

It is indeed a sterile nation,
a sterile world in which we live –
if it can still be called "living."
For we are entrenched in a culture of death
where life has lost its meaning.

Death is the answer to every problem,
and so sterility is the solution to all;
for if all were sterile
there would be no life,
and so no problem anymore.

How we fear newness of life!
The freshness of a new day,
a new breath from above…
We want no newborn babies,
nor the Spirit that gives them life.

It is curious, is it not,
that he who ostensibly celebrated life,
the hippie in all his glory,
ends inevitably embracing death…
though it may still seem like life to him?

Hippie Convert (I)

Here is the blindness again:
a man stands in a sterile wasteland
but is so lost in fantasy
that his head simply cannot see
the emptiness at his feet.

Beyond his feet
the emptiness creeps
and fills all from head to toe,
from the clouds in the sky
to earth and sea below.

And though it utterly surrounds him,
though he is thoroughly immersed in it,
still he thinks it is life he celebrates
and not the exultation
of his own desires.

It is a sad state, certainly,
and one not easily remedied:
how can mankind reclaim its dignity
when it closes its eyes
to the sacredness of life?

4. The Sacredness of Life

Life is sacred.
This is what all should see,
if they have eyes,
if their vision has not been polluted…
if they are what they were meant to be.

Some may say, "What of priests and nuns,
who do not have children;
are they not refusing life?"
But these give due reverence
to the creative power of man.

They do not seek their own pleasure
but offer it as a sacrifice,
making themselves a holocaust at the service of all,
not denying life
but nourishing it with all their hearts.

Theirs is not sterility artificially conceived
but celibacy engendering purity.
It enables them best to see
the sacredness of life
and cherish it entirely.

Hippie Convert (I)

There is hope the hippie will realize this,
and more than one has sought religious life,
taking the desire for love
that overwhelms their souls
and channeling it to a chaste call.

Then the birds' song becomes clear,
ringing with morning purity;
and the flowers bloom in innocence,
opened by the breath of God.
By lust they are no longer marred.

How freeing is this blessed embrace
of chastity for the LORD's sake,
for thus the LORD comes
to dwell in one's heart…
and with such a lover nothing could compare.

It is like pure, white clouds
in a clear blue sky:
a surpassing peace envelops the soul.
To this peace there is no end,
and by it no one is harmed.

John Lennon proclaimed peace
and said, "Imagine there's no Heaven."
But how can there be peace
if the place of peace, home of the Prince of Peace,
does not exist?

It is a man-made peace
of which he speaks,
and this is no peace at all;
it is selfish and vain
as man himself.

John Lennon proclaimed love
but beat his wife
and used scores of young women
as tools for his pleasure:
adultery and fornication are not love.

I realized the hypocrisy of this one day
as I looked at my dad and mom.
I had been taught to scorn such faithfulness…
but love was with these two
who remained faithful fifty years and more.

Hippie Convert (I)

John Lennon declared
the Beatles more popular than Christ,
and in this he did not lie;
for indeed they had captured the hearts
of millions of impressionable youth.

And such possession of soul
by the idols of the world
stays with many throughout their lives:
they grow only further from the truth
and deeper into fantasy.

In the end Lennon seemed to awaken,
making "God bless our love"
one of his final lyrics.
And for his sake let us hope he was wrong
about the presence of Heaven.

For he is dead now,
along with other prophets
who looked only to this world for peace.
But this world will end
and, with them, exist no more.

And so, let us not throttle
the sacredness of life
and the transcendent nature of peace;
if there is nothing surpassing our understanding,
there is no hope anymore.

But as it is there is the glow
of a woman at peace
with her pregnancy;
and the child she brings forth
shines with the newness of God's majesty.

Of such is the Kingdom of God,
the children who know the LORD and love,
who do not deny their blessings
and turn instead
to drugs and sex.

Innocence is all
and it will carry us home;
it never leaves the patient soul
who will be brought thereby
to the glory of Heaven.

5. The Glory of Heaven

The glory of Heaven
is not like the artificial lights
that shine in this world,
the glamorous ideologies that capture
corrupted minds and souls.

The glory of Heaven
shines with a purity and truth
that cannot be imitated
by the instruments men make,
by the theories they proclaim.

The hippie cannot see this
but is rather caught up
in a false sense of glory,
a dying, pretentious light.
The devil tries always to seem like Christ.

And it is the devil
that leads his heart astray.
It does not seem so to a culture
so used to his wiles, his ways…
but evil manufactures the idols of this age.

World peace is nice to think of,
but when it requires the killing
of those who are inconvenient to its goals,
who do not walk lockstep in its path,
is it really desirable at all?

They come speaking of peace and love,
but to achieve their idea of these
they will sacrifice peace
and redefine love
as they see fit.

For men's hearts cannot wait
for the blossoming of true love and peace;
they cannot consider the sacrifice
needed to sense them in this place…
They would take matters in their own hands.

A flower here, a flower there,
it all seems very beautiful –
but point out that the flower wilts
and their hands will cover their ears,
and they will soon rush upon you like Stephen.

Hippie Convert (I)

But Stephen saw the glory of Heaven;
it was this fact
that caused his persecutors
to pounce upon him –
it was simply too much for them to bear.

But he saw the glory of Heaven
and declared it to all,
unafraid of the consequences…
and with forgiveness of his killers
upon his lips.

Into the LORD's hands
he commended his spirit,
much like Jesus Himself.
His spirit was joined to Christ's own,
and so he knew the glory of Heaven.

This is the peace all should seek:
the peace that endures beyond death,
the love that cannot be quenched
even by torture –
this peace comes from God alone.

The peace of Christ be with you, my brother.
His peace fill your soul.
Then you shall indeed draw near to Him;
then you will be the LORD's own.
This peace is all that has worth.

There is a hippie who has come to see this,
who has found the peace
he sought so vainly.
The emptiness and insanity that was all around him
has been cast far from his soul.

Now a genuine peace breathes within him;
now a true love beats in his heart.
He has been converted from vanity
to the fullness of God's light…
and every day draws closer to His side.

In the Eucharist especially
he has found this peace;
in the truth of the LORD's presence
he makes his home –
and it cannot be taken from him.

6. Conversion

How blessed is he now!
And not only to be free
of drugs and fornication –
though how sweet that freedom is! –
but to be in the heart of the Church.

It is almost impossible to imagine,
considering where he had been
and how polluted he had become,
that he should now be clean,
indeed, free to sing the praises of God.

How can it be he is in church every day,
and every day receiving the Sacrament?
How can it be
he spends hours each day in prayer,
and has done so for years?

He is blessed beyond words,
free from all bonds
to the world and all it holds.
Though far from perfect, with a long way to go,
he has come in truth to a place of freedom.

Two Books

Perhaps it is not so impossible.
He was raised Catholic after all,
and though he understood none of it,
he did always sense the presence of Jesus,
even in the midst of his sin.

He could not imagine Jesus is not God;
it would be like saying he has no fingers
or doesn't breathe the air,
so undeniable was this truth to him.
And so I suppose his conversion does make sense.

He always had been a quiet soul,
contemplative by nature,
and so the spiritual life suited him.
But he had doubted every teaching
the Church proposed.

Who is this Pope,
and what is this "one Church"?
How dare they assert such authority!
And shouldn't we rebel against the powers that be,
for look at what corruption is there?

Hippie Convert (I)

Let us rather be free
to do as we please –
isn't Jesus full of compassion for all?
This adolescent spirit was strong in him,
for it was truth he sought.

Of course, truth without wisdom
is not worth much,
and can indeed be a detriment to truth;
it becomes a blunt instrument,
like the one rebelled against.

And so, much the man needed to learn;
very far he had to go.
But conversion came to his soul,
and eventually he welcomed it whole…
and became a model Catholic.

It is in this House truth rests;
the Spirit is upon this bark.
Peter we need to steer us to port,
lest, adrift at sea,
we get dashed upon the rocks.

Two Books

But as he sits daily in the adoration chapel,
still it is remarkable to him
that he is here,
so close to the Lord and His Church…
so much at peace in His presence.

One could say it comes with age,
but his conversion began by twenty-two,
and though it took a decade
before he came truly into the Church,
it has been decades he has been home again.

One can't say this hippie
ever consciously, knowingly rebelled
or left the House of God…
As with all hippies, he just drifted along
wherever the tide seemed to take him.

Today they say, "It's all good,"
no matter how bad it may be;
then we said, "It's cool,"
without thinking…
and so all sort of things entered in.

Hippie Convert (I)

The thing that mostly entered in
was the lyrics of songs
repeated ad infinitum
and so training his mind
to think in a certain way.

Not all were terrible
and some were good,
or could at least be taken positively…
but on the whole the message was one
of doing what one will.

They painted a picture of a corrupted world –
and the world is indeed corrupt.
But their solution was just as corrupt,
though couched in altruistic terms.
The singers were no better than the Pharisees.

These artists were often as filthy rich
as those they condemned for their money;
and the adulation they received
had no compare,
and so could not have been more troubling.

Two Books

How great is the hypocrisy
of those who condemn the washing of hands
yet care not for the filth upon their souls.
They are equally as contemptible
as those advocating vain washing.

It is not the washing of hands
that should concern any man
but the purity of his heart
and the love he bears
his fellow man.

But one does not love the soul he condemns,
and only thereby condemns himself;
for no man is above the law
or without merit for condemnation…
though all men think themselves so.

The hands to the throat of one's enemy
serve only to strangle oneself.
What will raise us from such futility;
who will save us
from dying in pride and pretense?

7. Salvation

We will only be saved
by the one who cries out our sins
like John the Baptist to Herod,
like Jesus to the soul of every man –
it is only the truth that will set us free.

But the cry must come
from a heart of love,
a heart concerned for the salvation
of the one to whom it speaks,
else all shall die in judgment.

He who cries out without love
condemns himself in his judgment,
and he will never serve
to convert the soul of the other…
who will thus likewise die in his sin.

But the truth must be spoken
and spoken with strength –
all men must be called to repentance.
Ignorance of sin will not save us
but only encourage the path to destruction.

Two Books

Salvation or condemnation,
these are the only two options.
We will be saved or we will be condemned;
and likewise we offer others
salvation or condemnation.

And so we must each check our soul
to see if love of the other
we have at heart,
or if we ride on a high horse
as the hippie so often does.

Never trust anyone over 30
was the foolish theme of the hippie generation;
thereby he condemned as useless
anyone not like himself,
presuming thus that he knew best.

But we must first distrust ourselves
and the judgment we invoke.
One would hope the hippie
might at least heed his own words
as his decades go well past three.

Hippie Convert (I)

But even at 70
the hippie remains angry at others
and blind to his own sin.
What hope for salvation can there be
for a fool full of years?

Foolishness can almost be expected,
certainly more easily understood,
in the young who are ignorant.
But ignorance in old age
is an obstacle difficult to surmount.

Particularly if the blindness is willful,
it grows harder with age,
for the soul becomes more self-assured
it is traveling the right way…
and who can tell it anything then?

But those called to cry out in love
must continue regardless of results:
it is not up to them to judge
the reception they get
but always to hold out hope to all.

Two Books

We know that salvation comes
only by the blood of Christ,
but so many cannot see this
and so rely only
on their own mind and will.

Some mock such an idea;
some see no need for salvation at all,
or at least not their own.
We know that salvation comes from Christ,
but many cannot or will not see this truth.

And so, what does the devout soul do?
How does he relate to the unbelief
and even antagonism
of those who reject the faith we know?
Salvation comes by the blood of Christ.

We must be ready to die,
to give our lives for those
who make themselves our enemies,
and enemies of the Lord.
We must wholeheartedly embrace the Cross.

Hippie Convert (I)

This is the sign of a genuine Christian;
this is the way we know
our conversion is becoming complete:
if we are ready to die
for the salvation of those who hate us.

This is Christ's message,
this is His call
and the way He showed us to walk.
It is indeed what He did,
and so a Christian can only do the same.

When the hippie thinks no more of himself,
of what he wants and desires,
what benefits him most
and what he thinks is right,
then he begins to grow in faith.

Then salvation is on the horizon
for him and for those around him,
for then he begins to live
not for himself
but for the good of all.

8. The Good of All

In love and peace we are all to live –
is this not the cry of the hippie?
Everybody love one another;
let there be no more war…
Let the flowers grow, man!

And James came to realize
that this overriding ideal
of the hippie movement
was fulfilled in Jesus Christ.
All else is a pale imitation.

Only in Jesus is love, only in Jesus is peace –
I think I've said this before,
but it bears continual repetition:
God is love, true love,
and only in Him peace is found.

Heaven is where the good of all
is truly known;
and Heaven comes to earth now,
for Jesus walks among us…
and we must walk along with Him.

Hippie Convert (I)

If we truly care about the good of all
and not our own selfish concerns,
then we must know that the good of all
is found only in the One
who is Goodness itself.

And those who seek the truth,
who really desire the good of all,
cannot but know, do know,
the goodness found in God alone
and the union of all mankind in Him.

Otherwise we are distracted;
we are living an illusion
if we fail to see this truth,
if our hearts do not generously seek
the good of all souls.

For apart from Him
we will designate some
as unworthy of being called
into the ranks where the good of all
is measured by human judgment.

And so, some, if not many,
will inevitably suffer,
will inevitably be persecuted
for not fitting the definition
of those deserving the treatment of the good.

Men will thus be in the place of God,
who in the end separates sheep from goats.
They would make this separation now
according to their own thinking,
their own will to power.

But in the end they will be powerless
before the One who judges all with Justice,
whose mercy pours down
like a river from Heaven
upon those who welcome such a gift.

Those who need not mercy,
who harden their hearts against His love,
cannot receive the mercy
they are so unwilling to give…
and they will not know the good of all.

Hippie Convert (I)

And so the hippie passes the peace pipe,
he takes another toke of his joint
and dreams of a world
where all live as one…
but he knows not that he is dreaming.

He thinks this cloud of smoke is reality,
and it is for him for a short while.
This is where he lives and breathes free…
but the air he breathes is not clear:
there is poison in it.

But this poison in his lungs
he does not recognize,
till it takes over his mind
and leaves him stultified,
unable to face down the paranoia.

It does us no good to live in a dream,
to seek to escape our problems
in whatever way we may conceive.
For the problems will only
come rushing upon us with greater force.

We cannot really be concerned
for the good of all
if we care not for the good of our own lives;
if we are not holy and healthy ourselves,
we will bring no good to anyone else.

It is only in the hand of God
we find the meaning of our lives,
the good all men are made for.
If we do not live in His grace,
no good can come to us.

And if there is no good in us,
indeed, what good can we be to others?
What good can we bring to the world
if we are mired in its corruption?
All but wilt in such a state.

The petals of a flower
is what we are
to the living LORD and God.
He cares immensely for the good of all
and calls us to nurture our brothers.

II.

1. Biography

I have mentioned few specifics of my own life
as I have expounded in general
about the hippie milieu
and the dangers present therein –
I suppose his sins are not unlike any man's.

And when I say "his sins"
I refer of course to my own,
and in this manner
compose a story of my life…
Still, perhaps I should become more particular.

One hesitates, of course,
to speak of oneself,
especially when the things one must say
are not very flattering
(though flattering words I would fear as well).

And so I must stop to pray
that the LORD will allow to be said
what He would have said,
and let silence remain where it should.
LORD, you are my surety in this.

Two Books

James strayed far from the presence of God
without ever realizing where he was going
until it was too late
and he found himself in a strange town
with no direction home.

It all happens little by little, really,
though there are milestones along the way.
The influence of music and lyrics
leads to interest in sex and drugs
and eventually the practice follows.

The practice increases
and grows in intensity
till one is quite addicted to sin,
though of this addiction
one remains unaware.

Then one day a ray of light
pierces through
and we glimpse our desperate state.
Conversion does not come all at once,
and so our only hope is patience.

Hippie Convert (II)

But how wonderful conversion is!
Even if there is considerable pain,
even if one must wait…
even if one is wrapped in darkness
with no apparent escape.

This darkness is far more desirable
than the darkness of sin,
for that darkness debilitates
whereas this darkness is but a prelude
to birth into new life.

Is this not what we find,
all those subject to conversion?
Whether we be hippies or squares,
the dark night must come upon all
who seek the Kingdom of God.

For the darkness of sin spares none
(save Our Lady),
and so it must be purged from us –
and this purgation, even here,
involves a certain suffering.

But, again, how blessed the suffering is!
And James felt this as deeply as any
for he had fallen as deeply as any
into the darkness of sin,
and so knew well the need for suffering.

There is great cleansing that comes
from the tears we cannot but cry
when our sins are raised
before our eyes
and we see them clearly.

How blessed are the tears,
how blessed is the recognition
of our faults,
of the depth of our sin…
and the lifeline Jesus throws us.

You must know what I mean, my brother.
You must have experienced this grace.
Could there be anything more blessed
than the forgiveness
of even our darkest sins?

Hippie Convert (II)

And so, suffering should be embraced
for the fruit it brings
to our lives
and the lives of those for whom we pray,
for whom we suffer.

Yes, our suffering can benefit
more than ourselves,
it can serve to purge more than our own souls,
if it is united with that of Christ,
who suffered always for others.

His suffering leads to glory,
to His own glory now in Heaven
where He reigns supreme,
and to the glory of any soul
that suffers with Him on this plane.

And so, though James regretted all his sin
(and, one must say, still does),
he rejoiced in the fruit his suffering brought
to the very depths of his heart,
a heart that had been so broken.

2. Broken Heart

The LORD looks upon the brokenhearted,
and so He looked upon James,
whose heart, whose life,
had been so broken by sin…
but was then healed by repentance.

I want to speak of the sin
that broke his heart,
that broke down his dignity
so gradually but so completely…
but still I do not know where to begin.

It is true I have spoken of the music
and even mentioned a couple of names…
but this barely scratches the surface
of his immersion in drugs and sex
and his blindness to the light of Christ.

Light of Christ was the name of the prayer group
that served to finally lift him forever
from the sin of cohabitation,
but this was three decades along in his life…
and still the spirit of fornication was not banished.

Hippie Convert (II)

The drugs were conquered much sooner,
even in his early twenties;
there was but a single toke of a joint
a few years after that…
and this demon has not raised its head again.

It took possession of him in earnest
when he was only 15:
after hearing so long of the sweetness of the leaf
and the enlightenment from LSD,
he bought his first bag of dope.

He smoked it alone
in the park where he had grown
and played as a child.
He rolled his first joint incorrectly
in a cellar infested with photos of nudes.

There he had discovered pornography years before
(as early as age nine or ten),
and it had become a constant pastime;
now he had begun another vice,
one which would quickly take over his life.

Two Books

He soon was smoking marijuana or hashish
every day, usually twice a day (or more),
and taking mescaline or acid
on the weekends.
It was what he lived for.

And he started to grow his hair long
and put those patches on his jeans,
and attend any number of rock concerts.
Back in the 70's nobody cared
where or when drugs were taken…

So we smoked pot in Washington Square Park
or on the streets or in graveyards…
Only once near school
were we accosted by a cop,
but he let us go with a warning.

There was one policeman in the neighborhood
for whom we had to look out –
he was on a personal mission to bust kids –
but on the whole security was lax,
and so there was really no one to stop us.

Hippie Convert (II)

And James didn't seem at all broken:
he had become rather popular
and was now quite adept
at recognizing what was cool
and following the latest trends.

But the emptiness of this time was growing
as gradually he lost his own identity;
it was only being cool
that preoccupied him,
and saying and doing what cool people do.

In its social acceptance
how is one to recognize one's emptiness?
If all around are more or less empty,
who can tell the difference?
Anyone who was not empty didn't matter.

Those "squares" were souls to be ridiculed
for their ignorance of what mattered,
for their terrible ordinariness.
It was cool to burn oneself out with drugs –
those who rusted into old age were useless.

There were glimpses of reality through the haze,
senses of what it was to be wholesome,
and that this was not a foolish thing…
but remembrances of childhood and family life
were rather quickly dispelled.

What could one do but sex and drugs?
What mattered but rock 'n' roll?
School was something he took care of,
and he would regularly get money from his parents
for making the honor roll…

But that money was used for drugs,
as was the dollar provided for lunch.
All was geared toward getting high;
that was all anyone would do.
There was nothing more important than this idol.

But as all idols are empty,
so is the soul that follows them.
And the brokenness cannot be hidden forever,
or one would find oneself in hell.
Only its recognition can set us free.

Hippie Convert (II)

Peeling back the layers of darkness,
the mask that had so covered his heart,
James somehow began to breathe once more
and light began to touch his eyes.
He began to see that he was blind.

His heart beat again,
and blood coursed through his veins…
And that love still exists
he began to understand.
But in the process he was torn by pain.

As his conversion took hold
he renounced the things of this world,
especially the milieu of rock 'n' roll –
selling or giving all his albums away…
but also his books and whatever else he owned.

And then freedom came;
though he cried every night
for the sin still in his heart
and in his memory…
how sweet was the freedom that came.

3. Still Bound

Though there were distinct struggles
in conquering the demon of drugs –
once he threw a bag of marijuana
out a second-floor window,
vowing never to partake again…

And though he returned even after that
(he never bought drugs again
but did often and wholeheartedly
join in with others around him getting stoned),
a decisive end soon came, as has been said.

But the break was not so clean
with the spirit of fornication.
Of this there sometimes seems
no complete end, no final victory on this earth…
though it may be substantially overcome.

The reach of this spirit
was so deeply ingrained in his memory –
exposed to pornography at such a young age.
And since sex is so fundamental to our nature,
its perversion can be particularly severe.

Hippie Convert (II)

And so James found himself
still bound to it,
still faltering into it,
well after his initial time of repentance,
and even after his conversion to the Church.

It is remarkable the excuses
the human mind can make,
the way it can smooth over
even the most obvious (and grave) sins –
and how tragic it is to trust our own judgment!

Once a priest said quite simply in Confession
that it was not right for him
to live with a woman outside marriage
or to have relations with anyone thus…
but he could only argue they would one day marry.

But they never did marry,
and later – upon receiving the Spirit's grace –
it became clear to him
how wrong the relationship had been,
and how very wrong he was.

And this incident was by no means isolated,
nor was it the final one.
Though he never lived with a woman
or engaged in coitus again,
still he made excuse for sexual sin.

Eventually he began to run to Confession
each time he fell into sin;
and though he may have been sincere
at the time of each penance,
all too soon he would fall again.

It was very much like a demon
had a hold of him,
something almost beyond his control.
Then there were those who made excuse for him…
and he was certainly ready to listen.

We hear what we want to hear
and ignore the rest
when truth hasn't really taken hold of our soul,
when, as St. Augustine said,
we tell the LORD, "Yes, but not now."

Hippie Convert (II)

We tell ourselves we are in love –
how terribly that word is misused! –
and so presume to know what we do…
but love is something of which we have no sense,
though we are well acquainted with lust.

Or at least vain fantasy,
a relationship we invent in our minds;
and if someone says we have no clothes,
we think it must be they
who refuse to see the truth.

Thank God James came to see the truth
any number of times;
it was very unfortunate
he repeatedly fell into blindness,
but by grace he was continually raised.

It is not an easy path to walk,
especially when everyone else
speaks so confidently of "love"
and encourages us along the way.
But, still, the blindness we must conquer.

Two Books

We cannot blame others
for our falling into sin,
no matter how much they influence us,
no matter how guilty they may be –
we must take responsibility when we stray.

For it is *our* feet that take the steps,
our heart that gives its assent,
and it is we who are thereby afflicted…
and so it is we who must seek a cure.
It does no good to point to others' disease.

All are so sick and in need of a physician!
The society has a cancerous sore.
The question is who will face
his own immorality,
his own turning away from the light of the LORD.

May the LORD come to heal us;
may we beg His assistance.
May we see that our salvation is beyond us
and call out for the hand of God.
Only He can keep us from sinking into the deep.

4. The Cesspool

We may have all jumped
into the cesspool together,
we may have celebrated
our liberation as a whole…
but we must be pulled out one by one.

The LORD will judge each individual soul;
we will have to give account of our lives
alone before His face.
And then what shall we say?
We will not be able to excuse ourselves that day.

It is true,
the pull of the cesspool is very strong.
There is no question
that the culture would carry us away…
but we can't be dead bodies floating downstream.

We must fight against the tide –
this is where we will find our lives.
We prove our worth
and the purpose of our breath
by how we stand up against evil.

Two Books

Who was able to recognize
the mud that swamped
the ground at Woodstock
as a cesspool rising
beneath our feet?

Who could have predicted
how deep we would sink?
This was our way back to the Garden,
back to innocence and truth…
not the dawning of an age so bleak.

And who can see it now?
How many still wear
rose-colored glasses
and hide themselves
behind a wall of smoke and ash?

But as the ash heap rises,
as the death toll mounts,
how long will they be able
to convince themselves
that this is the way to Paradise?

Hippie Convert (II)

How could we be so fooled?
Why do we not say,
"My God, what have I done?"
Why do we turn our eyes
from the enveloping sin?

How are we able to rationalize
the burning and dismemberment
of the most innocent among us
as the right of a woman
to do with her body as she pleases?

How can we institutionalize
relationships between man and man
and woman and woman,
equating them with marriage
as it has existed from the beginning?

How can we be so blind?
It is true that as the cesspool
creeps in and surrounds us
we can lose all sense of truth –
but still the will must give its assent.

The depths of the cesspool
are not known to the many
who avert their eyes in ignorance
of the prevalent horror,
and so it gains strength and greater depth.

There is a clarion call to convenience
that lulls the souls of all
to sleep, to ease,
to addiction to comfort –
and it seems nothing can penetrate such apathy.

They prefer not to see,
not to know the truth
of the way their leaders promote
the end of civilization,
the sinking into the cesspool.

Perhaps they do not know their complicity –
the ability to ignore or excuse
the consequences of our actions
is truly remarkable in man…
but always we are responsible for what we do.

Hippie Convert (II)

But who is responsible;
who even cares if they support
the killing of the unborn
or the leading of impressionable youth
into sexual and moral malaise?

And do not think the LORD will be appeased
when we say, "But we helped our neighbor."
Do not think He can be
as ignorant of evil
as we are wont to be.

He knows the depths of the cesspool.
He sees the complicity of souls.
And unless we repent,
when the end comes
our sins will be dreadfully raised to our eyes.

But if there is no sin,
why not continue on,
why not persist in ignoring
the blood rising, the disease spreading…
the lost generation of man?

And the greatest woe is of course
that the filth has entered the Church,
that even here refuge is threatened.
Yes, there is still light in this House,
and it continues to grow…

But the darkness has also found space
in this place where darkness
should never be,
in the abode of the LORD on earth –
it, too, has its human side.

Nothing will ever conquer the Spirit;
the darkness cannot overcome the light:
a purity ever remains in these walls
which the cesspool cannot reach.
But still the devil does what he can.

And even priests and bishops
go along with him,
fooled by their own weakness and sin,
giving in to the blindness that pervades this age…
We can only pray for them.

Hippie Convert (II)

And let us pray for our own souls,
that we will be purged of any filth
and preserved from its clutches
as the darkness closes in.
The way to the Kingdom is indeed narrow.

James struggled much
to lift himself out of the cesspool,
to free himself of its filth…
and though still he is far from perfect,
God's grace is at work in him.

It has helped that he has married
a woman seeking the LORD as he,
for whom faith is most important
and not the world's security.
He is not alone anymore.

And he is not so bound to the sin
that held him fast for so many years;
now with his wife there is a breath of peace,
a certain relief from anxiety
and the whisperings of the devil in his ear.

5. Death

Death is prescribed by the LORD
as a remedy for man's sin,
for his succeeding misery.
The LORD wills the death of no man,
but man's disobedience makes it necessary.

How shall we attain to the glory
the LORD intends for all
if we remain forever in the darkness
of this forsaken world?
It simply cannot be.

And so death is provided
as a release from the bonds
that chain us to the darkness,
that keep us in our sin.
All of this must be left behind.

And we must trust in the LORD,
in His power and will for our good.
For it will certainly seem
as if all is lost –
but by Him all is redeemed.

Hippie Convert (II)

Even the flowers wilt and die;
the sun shall rise and set
no more.
On that day we will clearly see
the illusion of peace we have devised.

When the glamour passes,
when its deception is revealed –
when the emptiness of our platitudes
can no longer be ignored,
how great the pain will be.

All that we set our hearts upon,
all the selfishness we conceived,
will be seen for the nothingness
it truly is.
And what is true will be far away.

Why do we seek such emptiness?
Why mock obedience to God?
On the day we die we will see
we are not He…
Let us pray He does not flee from us.

Two Books

The end is certainly upon us.
Jesus is coming, and soon.
Then there will be no denying His presence;
there will be no hiding from His face.
And where will we be without His grace?

James came to know how close the LORD is,
how near is the end of all things
and the beginning of His Kingdom.
Repenting of his sin,
what really matters became evident to him.

And death was not so much to be feared anymore,
since he was not so attached
to the things that pass.
His sin he no longer treasured
but saw it as something to be cast aside.

This is the beginning of new life:
death to this world.
This brings the joy and peace
that passes understanding,
for then we know what does not pass away.

Hippie Convert (II)

We seem like fools,
we who do not pursue
the things of this world.
And our death seems a terrible affliction,
particularly for all we have missed.

If there is no resurrection of the dead,
truly we are the greatest of fools;
if there is nothing beyond this life,
what do we have,
we who sacrifice this life?

Nothing. Nothing at all.
We hold to nothing of this world,
and so if there is nothing but this world,
we have nothing at all.
But there is more than this world.

There is something living and true;
even in this place it is known to us.
And we shall have everything
when the nothingness of this world is gone
and only the LORD remains.

Then there will be love and peace
and flowers in abundance.
Then there will be no violence
on all the LORD's holy mountain.
Then the lamb will lie down with the lion.

But this will come through death,
not through the latest designer drug.
This will come only
in leaving the fantasies of the mind
distinctly behind.

All we imagine is good
falls short of the vision of God,
and so only by giving our vision to Him
will we find the desire of our hearts.
Only then will the band play as one.

And we will be as brothers and sisters,
and there will be no mud.
And we will hug one another
and greet each other with a kiss…
and the purity of the LORD will be with us.

III

1. The Garden

How shall we find our way back to the Garden?
We can't. We have destroyed it.
Both our souls and Creation itself
have been irreparably damaged.
And so the Garden exists no more.

And for those who set their sights
on Nature alone,
who cannot see beyond the horizon
or the trees before their noses,
things are thus quite hopeless.

If the Garden has been plundered,
if our souls have been polluted by sin,
if we have defaced the image of God
throughout Creation,
how shall we find a place of peace?

We have no home here on this earth;
our only home is in Heaven.
And the coming of that Kingdom
does not depend on the will of man.
It is a gift of God Most High.

Two Books

James came to understand
that all we must really do
is breathe for a living,
if that breath is of the Breath of God.
He will do the rest.

Seek ye first the Kingdom of God,
and all else will be added unto you –
James found this to be remarkably true
in his own life:
when we serve the LORD, all is provided.

We need not worry
or be anxious about anything –
we need but breathe and be at peace,
for, truly, He will take care.
The Garden is in our midst.

This is still God's Creation;
we cannot escape His presence anywhere.
Though much energy is spent
manufacturing darkness,
it is all as nothing in the end.

Hippie Convert (III)

A particular witness James could offer
regarding the providence of the LORD
are the blessings that came to him
when he began to tithe –
he never had a money worry afterward.

A new priest had come to the parish
who encouraged giving 5% to the Church
and 5% to other charities…
but James had only $200 in the bank
and very minimal wages.

But a friend had begun his tithe
despite being married with two young children
and work prospects less than his own.
So, inspired by that example,
he began tithing.

That was more than twenty years ago,
and the blessings could hardly be counted:
finding work when there seemed none,
considerable increases in wages,
apartments at very low cost…

Money and gifts seemed to come
from nowhere (and from everywhere),
as when more recently an insurance company
contacted his wife about policies about to expire,
ones she had forgotten she had.

The notice was mailed to an address
where she hadn't lived for twenty years,
but somehow arrived in their box 1200 miles away.
What comes when we practice poverty
and entrust our lives to the LORD!

There can be no more generous boss
than our Most Holy God,
who holds all the world in His hand
and seeks to share His favors with everyone:
those dedicated to Him live in His Garden.

He indeed cannot be outdone
in His tremendous generosity –
how often James found the more he gave,
the more he received in return…
until he had an abundance.

Hippie Convert (III)

He now has more the problem
of what to do with stored-up finances;
and though income is still needed
to meet certain requirements…
this too continues to come (as shown above).

I pray the LORD will bless you
with trust in Him and in His providence,
for this is truly the greatest of His gifts:
to know that indeed by Him
all the hairs of our head are counted.

Do not be anxious for tomorrow;
the troubles of the day are sufficient.
Look at the birds of the air
and the flowers of the field –
how they are cared for by the LORD!

And you are worth more than many sparrows;
learn simply to breathe
and you will be blessed.
Trust in Him even in your darkest hour,
and His great light you will know.

2. Exile

In His Garden there is ample food and clothing,
so why would anyone go anywhere else?
Why is man not satisfied
with what God provides?
Why does he wish to leave this place?

It is his own will
that casts man from the Garden;
it is his desire that is thus fulfilled.
The LORD wishes to keep him near –
He made the Garden especially for man.

But man turns selfishly away.
Lacking gratitude for God's gift
and without sense for what is good,
he prefers something other than love…
He chooses darkness over light.

It is indeed foolishness
to bite the hand by which we are fed,
to renounce the One
who has our interest at heart.
But this is what man does.

Hippie Convert (III)

He turns to so many things
that are less than God,
that lack of His undying love.
He prefers instead to die,
to lose the life planted in him.

And so he goes into exile;
so his heart becomes void.
Hardened like Pharaoh
against the voice of the LORD,
he even oppresses the children of light.

But it is he who is most oppressed,
he who is under slavery,
who cannot escape from exile…
for our only home is with the LORD
and those furthest from Him are most to be pitied.

Even in forced labor
the children of God remain free;
even under religious persecution
their faith stays strong,
and grows ever stronger.

Two Books

But the soul that rejects the LORD,
that in his pride turns from the Light
to make a light of his own invention,
to take life and death in his own hands…
what can he be but cast from the Garden?

Indeed, he casts himself out;
by his own choice he leaves.
What has become of the hippie soul
who fancied himself above it all,
above all human weakness?

He was to make a brave new world,
one transcending all man's flaws.
On a mountaintop he set himself,
looking down on all the peasants below…
but how far into the pit he has fallen!

Now he embraces the culture of death
and the ideology of the superior man –
there are many he sees as expendable
(the child in the womb, the disabled, the old…),
and so he has exiled himself from humanity.

Hippie Convert (III)

Exiled where he stands,
a foreigner in his own skin,
he seeks to shed the flesh
that he might find freedom.
(Thus he justifies the killing of others as well.)

He seeks an escape,
a way outside of himself…
but finds no exit.
He tries drugs, alcohol, sex,
and the current fad of the passing day.

But nothing satisfies,
nothing brings joy to his soul;
for he has renounced the source of joy,
the source of truth and innocence,
and the love that is life itself.

He needs no God,
sees Him as but a fantasy –
and so his life becomes a fantasy,
a pale imitation of the reality
that is life in the Garden.

Two Books

And in his stubbornness,
in his prideful despair,
he remains apart from God.
There is, of course, also fear,
fear that He might exist.

For then he himself would be called to life,
called to walk according
to the LORD and His ways,
and so have to abandon
the path to which he has grown accustomed.

And he would have to face his sin,
that there are actually things he's done wrong,
things that require atonement.
He cannot imagine himself on his knees
before anything or anyone.

For certainly he knows best –
what trust he has in his own mind!
He gives no thought
to whence his mind has come
or the One who made him.

Hippie Convert (III)

How he cherishes his despair
and the relief it seems to give him
from carrying any cross.
It is easier this way…
one hardly has to think.

There is sloth in his pride,
an unwillingness to do the work
necessary to address the truth
and live in its presence.
He does not wish to be set free.

There is fear, too,
that it might not be real,
like so many things he has found unreal;
he fears another illusion
will overtake his soul.

But we cannot fear the darkness
or run in an effort to escape,
for then it indeed takes hold of us,
as is its evil purpose.
Face the darkness and let it pass through!

Pity the poor lost hippie
who knows not which way to turn,
who clings so tenaciously
to the illusions of his youth,
to the blindness he refuses to see.

He is but a part
of the overarching culture
and its insistent call
to do as we please.
The selfishness encompasses all.

The child that never grows up,
that remains spoiled all his life…
pity him for he knows not the beauty
of self-sacrifice,
of the love to which all souls are called.

And so he lives in exile,
far apart from his true self –
he rejects being a child of God
in favor of some useless ideal,
and so he toils quite alone.

3. The Spirit of the Age

How easily, and readily,
we confuse the spirit of the age
with the Spirit of God.
Both are of the spirit, of course,
but they are usually polar opposites.

And this confusion has perhaps never been greater
and more troubling
than it is in our own day,
when people think that all they do
is in the will of God, their Maker.

There is no sense of sin anymore,
no need for repentance,
for we have made our own perfection,
or rather baptized all we do
as inherently blessed.

And such foolish blasphemy
is taught even in some Catholic schools,
where impressionable students are told
whatever they think is right,.
with no recognition of the evil this brings.

Two Books

There is certainly a difference
between the will of God
and our own conscience,
for the conscience must be formed
and conformed to the mind of Christ.

If not it cannot be Christian;
if not it is not of God.
And this formation does not occur naturally –
we are more inclined to wickedness
than the spirit of self-sacrifice.

It is the spirit of the age
to which we more readily listen;
it surrounds us all the time, after all,
and is followed by the rest of the world…
Why should we not go along?

And it easily becomes our god.
Without our even realizing,
we follow it without reserve.
It enters into our eyes and ears
and we become as its children.

Hippie Convert (III)

We are indeed its offspring,
for it forms our minds and hearts
and makes us who we are:
our very identities are inextricably linked
with this pervasive culture.

And it is indeed a culture of death,
a culture that kills the life of the soul,
destroying not only the unborn, sick, and elderly,
but all whom it embraces
and who embrace it without reserve.

But how can this be?
Surely I exaggerate?
What we see on TV is innocuous,
is it not?
The media is our friend.

And all our friends watch and listen attentively
to that which is widely proclaimed
for the consumption of the masses…
and the masses swallow it whole
without a thought for their souls.

Two Books

Should we not embrace homosexuality,
which appears so natural and fun?
Should we not remain silent
in the face of abortion,
understanding the rights of the woman?

Should we not accept that many people
are simply better off dead?
And should we not help them along that path,
especially if they are depressed?
Where would our compassion be otherwise?

We could not go against the tide
even if we wanted to;
it is just too overwhelming.
There is left no choice –
our wills have been stripped from us.

And so we float with resignation,
if not joyful acceptance,
downstream with the dying things…
There is no time to stop and think
or question our presumed compassion.

Hippie Convert (III)

And so the spirit of the age takes hold
and becomes the new religion,
one which must be abided
by all who live under its rule…
All must offer their pinch of incense.

For the idols of the age are jealous gods
who will countenance no compromise –
the word of these gods must be heeded.
And if you dare to speak up,
you will be thrown into prison.

And as the climate grows worse
for all who believe in the LORD,
ironically those who oppress the believers
become more confident they are doing right:
their hearts harden beyond remedy.

They are sure the "love" they profess
is true and full of reason;
they excuse their persecution
as necessary to protect their definition
of love as license to sin.

"Make love, not war."
This is the battle cry
of the hippie generation.
Of course what it means
is to have as much sex as you like.

The equating of love and sex
is perhaps the greatest tragedy
of these lost years.
O what the sexual revolution has wrought!
Broken hearts, broken lives, dead bodies…

In this war how many have died?
As I write this, nearly *60 million* unborn children
have been legally killed in the U.S.A. alone.
Is this not where "free love" leads –
does it not cost human lives?

And what of the broken marriages,
the broken families, the lost children…
We wonder from where
the pervasive violence comes –
has not this "love" led to such destruction?

Hippie Convert (III)

And the emptiness of this spirit,
the void in the soul of man…
how shall it be filled?
Not by further sinking into the pit.
Only by turning to the LORD of true love.

But it is our backs we turn to Him,
not our faces:
our heels are raised to run from Him.
And so how can He embrace us
who want no part of Him?

We have our religion set,
and it is set against God.
It seems right in our own eyes,
and we are the enlightened ones.
(Perhaps some shall see this is a creed of death.)

LORD, have we not always been the same,
always more ready to oppose you
than to praise you,
always sure that we know best,
blind to our selfishness?

4. Innocence

It is only innocence that will save us,
a genuine innocence,
a purity of heart…
not the childishness that suffuses
the culture of this age.

The LORD is perfectly innocent;
He is childlike and pure,
humble and lowly, obedient in soul…
and we must be like Him
to know innocence at all.

The culture pretends to know Him;
in fact, it presumes to be Him.
But what it knows is indeed a false light,
one opposed to purity and obedience,
one wrought in the filth of this world.

The hippie flashes the smile of a child,
acts indeed so innocently…
but his heart is set on fornication
and the high he can get from some drug –
no child desires these things.

Hippie Convert (III)

There is a beating heart within us all
that remembers the child we have been,
that recalls the love in which we were wrought
by the hand of the LORD.
And it invites us to return.

Here is where innocence dwells
as the solid foundation of all life,
as the substance of our souls.
God is the seed from which all is sprung
and that seed is planted in all of us.

Why do we cover it over with lies?
Why do we allow it
to become calloused and hard?
How is it we lose ourselves
in the evil of this world?

O the selfishness that corrupts our souls,
that separates us from the Spirit
to embrace rotting flesh…
Is this not utter foolishness?
Should we not come to our senses?

O the blessing of innocence,
the childlike spirit that enables us
to look with wonder upon the world,
upon ourselves and all around us
as if it were ever new.

And it is.
In the blood of Christ all is a miracle,
all is blessed by God's smile;
He looks down upon us as His children
and is greatly pleased when we look up at Him.

Then all is as it should be;
then the joy of life is fulfilled.
When we are children of our Father,
our joy is complete…
and He is joyful too.

Is it not miraculous
that we have ten fingers, ten toes,
that we breathe and our heart beats,
and our eyes are filled with light?
We are living in a miracle!

Hippie Convert (III)

This miracle cannot be known
by those whose hearts are corrupt,
whose souls are wrought with lies…
for their eyes are veiled,
covered over as by a crust.

There is still a soft heart somewhere within –
we cannot entirely kill the child we have been.
But how hard our exterior can become,
making the heart so very dull…
as if it exists not at all.

Separate yourself not from the innocent heart;
do not become so callous and jaded
that you know not the wonder anymore.
God is calling to you still,
whispering deep inside your soul.

See the false idols
to which you have sworn allegiance,
which have led you so far afield.
All things are good in their proper place,
but make no god of anything.

Two Books

How the hippie worships Nature,
bowing down before sun and moon;
seeking to live closer to the earth,
he sees not how it swallows him,
blinding his eyes to what is above.

There is something beyond the stars,
beyond the limitations of the universe.
Though all is made by the LORD
and blessed by His hands,
none of it can compare with Him.

Earth and sun and sky
are beautiful, wonderful to behold,
awe-inspiring in their majesty…
but in the end they are nothing
if they do not lead us to their King.

The LORD reigns over Heaven and earth,
and He rules our very souls.
He whose reach extends throughout Creation
makes His home in every heart.
Let us make a place for Him.

Hippie Convert (III)

It is in innocence we find our call,
we find who we really are:
as God's children alone are we free
to walk this earth in peace
and come at last to Heaven.

This world was made for us, my friend,
but we must be made (and remade) in God's image
if we are to receive this gift
He offers with a generous heart –
otherwise we will be quite lost.

There is no need to fear,
no need to doubt the love of the LORD
and the goodness in our souls.
It is in this goodness we must make our home;
then we will be dwelling with Him.

O LORD, touch every person you have made
with your tenderness, with your love.
In innocence, as your children,
let us remain all our days
and come quickly to your side.

5. At His Side

It is only at the side of the LORD
we find our home,
we take our rest in this world
and in the next.
There is no other place at all.

What good are any of our plans,
the things we pursue with such zeal,
if they are not founded in the LORD,
if they are not in His will?
They will but come to naught.

And so many things there are that distract us,
that take our attention from what matters.
We thus lose sight of what is important
and wander aimlessly
in our convicted ignorance.

We are so sure of ourselves,
so sure of the latest fad
devised by the princes of advertising
and the current knighted sage
who leads us in his ways.

Hippie Convert (III)

How ready we are to follow false paths,
how easily led astray,
for we would prefer to be anywhere else
than in the arms of the LORD this day.
What is it we are running from?

And what is it we are running to?
This we do not know.
All we know is we don't want the LORD –
let our anxiety take us where it will.
But we will never be successful.

There is no escaping our God
for we are always in His hands:
He is never far from us.
And however fast we run,
we will get no further from Him.

Only from ourselves.
We will flee only further
from who we are,
from our very souls…
and be left quite alone.

Does not inconstancy reign supreme
in our age of distractions?
We turn our attention from one thing
to whatever passes before our eyes…
We know not where we are going.

But we are moving quickly,
busy always with this or that.
There is so much to be busy with,
who can tend to his heart?
Who is concerned for the state of his soul?

We have our ideologies, certainly,
which provide a contrived sense of security –
secure they seem indeed (or so we make them),
but the ground is moving beneath our feet
for they are built on sand.

And we must not let the light of reason in
to question the flaws in our plans;
this above all we must not do,
for then what would become of our ideals?
To another idol we'd have to turn.

Hippie Convert (III)

It is a drug-ridden society;
such is our answer to everything.
It is in this haze we take refuge
from any weakness of body, mind, or soul…
And so our hearts are quite forlorn.

Can't you see the emptiness in all this?
Do not be afraid to face the darkness.
For then you will find the way out,
which is only by the grace of God.
Trust in Him and you will be saved.

Cease running away from Him;
turn and look upon His face.
Though your sins will be exposed in that light,
in that light they will also be forgiven.
And you will find true freedom.

Your slavery to the drugs that breed
only vain fantasy,
that only further poison your soul
and keep you from wholeness in the LORD,
must be cast far away.

But we would rather medicate ourselves
than fly to the side of the LORD
and come before Him as children.
We are adults and decide for ourselves,
and make for ourselves our own demise.

We cannot recognize the One greater than us,
by whose hand we were made;
we have no humility.
It is embarrassing even to think of Him,
to think of ourselves as His children.

But mostly it is fear that keeps us away,
fear borne in our sin
and our reluctance to admit it
and leave it far behind…
And so, how purity harrows us.

We cannot look upon His face,
we cannot come to His side…
but it is at His side
that we find our peace,
only here and no other place.

Hippie Convert (III)

Come to His side, my brother;
do not be afraid or ashamed.
He has only love for you –
accept the gift of His grace.
His arms He will place around you.

What comfort is there!
There, what a home we make.
Sparrows find a home in His altar
and here our soul is nourished well –
come to the hand that feeds you.

Step away for a moment
from your futile existence
and you will never wish to return;
come to your senses this day
and you will no longer fear tomorrow.

At your side we find our home, O LORD;
let us stay here with you forever.
At your side time is eternal:
your love exists always.
Even now you call us to be with you.

6. Freedom

What is there the hippie heart
and the human heart in general –
and especially the American heart –
desires more than freedom?
It is the core of the modern creed.

We've got to be free.
We've got to be able to do as we please…
and let no one question us.
But of course the freedom of which man speaks
is but a slavery.

In the license to do as we please
we find that what we please to do
leads to chained hands and feet,
spiritually for those who profess this creed,
and physically for those who oppose.

God help the soul who gets in the way
of this train with no conductor;
and God help most of all
those who travel upon it,
for truly their souls are lost.

Hippie Convert (III)

As there is no peace,
there is no freedom apart from God,
no means of centering our lives…
we are so free that we become lost,
traveling in a thousand directions at once.

And we have no control of ourselves,
no reason, no discerning faculty;
and so we are acted upon by outside forces,
which force us into slavery.
How can such a soul be free?

There is no wisdom here
where people do as they please;
how quickly their minds are darkened,
and how pitifully they grope in the dark.
But this they cannot see.

All they see is what they want,
what they think is best…
what pleases them most.
But how quickly that pleasure turns to a pain
from which they cannot escape.

Two Books

Only in God is anyone free,
for only He is truly free;
only He does what He wills
for He wills only good for all,
and only in goodness does freedom exist.

In evil is only slavery,
is only the death of the soul,
the life of man –
evil is like poison:
it makes us unable to breathe or move.

It moves us; it conquers us
and takes control of our hands and feet.
And so we go where it tells us
and reach out according to its demands.
Indeed, it would choke the very life from our souls.

Evil does not wish to see us thrive
but only to bow down before it and die.
God alone provides us with the freedom
to decide where we shall walk,
even if is on an evil path.

Hippie Convert (III)

Our sins are like little kings
invoking their rule over what we do.
They dictate to our hearts and minds
their wishes and desires,
and we can but obey.

How we fear to offend
the dictates of sin;
how trapped we are on the path
sin marks out for us.
It seems we have no choice but to follow its ways.

But God gives us a choice
to turn from sin and be redeemed.
He would break the chains of slavery
and breathe life into our souls again –
and how wonderful this freedom is!

Especially when one has been thoroughly bound
by one's participation in grave sin
(regardless of how willingly we entered therein) –
the taste of freedom is all the more glorious
the deeper the pit from which we emerge.

Two Books

And the pit is very deep today;
it seems unconquerable,
made especially so by our blind acceptance
of its presence in our lives –
we think this is simply the way it is.

But in this way we are not:
we surrender to the talons of death
and slide into nothingness.
But there is something other than nothingness –
there is the call of the LORD to live!

Though freedom may not come easily
because of our having been
so prone to the slavery
the world inevitably brings,
it still may be attained.

However deep we may have sunk,
however much we have lost our souls,
the LORD continues to call us home
and provides the grace to reach there
if we but turn and trust in Him.

Hippie Convert (III)

How many there are
who have come out of the darkness,
out of the pit the devil digs
to capture our souls, our very will,
and cover us over with dirt.

Up from the grave let us rise!
The LORD will dispel
the terrors of death
and bring us to new life…
O let us seek to arise!

I recall reclining on a couch one time
while in exile in San Francisco;
my hand I saw upon my head
but I sensed there would be nothing I could do
if my neck it should decide to strangle.

I've looked upon the rocks below
and the waves crashing upon them,
and I've leaned out over the edge
once or twice…
but pulled myself back again.

Two Books

We must have the will to live,
to leave the culture of death behind
and breathe fresh, clear air,
free of all the pollution of sin
and the lies to which the world subscribes.

There is always hope, my friend,
however long the path may be.
Choose to turn and walk toward the LORD
and He will draw you near Him.
And you will find the perseverance you need.

The father of the Prodigal Son
threw his arms around him,
running toward his ungrateful heir
even as he saw him from a distance…
And for this wretch he called a feast!

The days following may have been difficult
for the selfish young man
who had so embraced the darkness…
but the light never leaves us.
It remains always present to guide.

Hippie Convert (III)

And so, let us come
to the freedom found in God,
however long it takes to arrive there.
Let us not lose hope
but lose all that serves to diminish it.

What the heart of the hippie desires most
it will find in the presence of Jesus,
in the light of the Kingdom of God.
There all souls will join
in one harmonious song.

Praising the LORD is what sets us free
to be joyful all our days
with nothing to fear,
nothing to lose
anymore.

All given over to our God,
it is preserved unto eternity…
We shall ever have all we need.
For all we need is this freedom
found in the One LORD of all.

7. One

What does the hippie thirst for
more than the oneness of all?
For it is in this oneness
peace is found,
the peace of every living creature.

He seeks this oneness in illusory places,
in idols of one kind or another,
and so he is unable to find what he seeks...
But when he turns in faith to Christ,
the spirit of true oneness fills his mind.

And he sees as he walks down the street
that all the older women are his mother,
the younger ones his sisters,
and the men his father and brothers –
for all are one in Jesus.

The Father has only one Son
and those who are joined to Him
become as adopted children
loved by the Father as His own...
and this blessing they see in one another.

Hippie Convert (III)

And joy rings out from the heart of those
who see what the LORD has wrought,
that He has wrought us as His own
and calls us to join together
in the heart of His Beloved Son.

It does not matter our race
or the place of our birth;
of what consequence is the color of our skin
or the appearance of our hair,
how tall we are or how strong?

In those who seem most different than us
we find the greatest joy
when we discover the truth:
that they are indeed our brothers,
our mothers, our fathers, our sisters…

Let us long to rejoice in each other
in the love of God –
is this not the truest of love,
that which loves without condition,
that joins all souls together?

And there is only one language
in the presence of God:
we all speak with the same tongue
for we all speak of Christ's love.
What else is there to say?

And so, let us not be separated
as at the Tower of Babel
but join our voices in one chorus
of praise to our holy LORD.
In this we shall find our voice.

Flesh of His flesh and bone of His bone,
truly do we become one;
eating His Body and drinking His Blood,
who can we be but Him?
And He is certainly One.

Let Jesus' blood course through our veins;
in His skin let us make our home…
and not only will we be one
with Him and with one another,
but with all of Creation as well.

Hippie Convert (III)

The earth will sing out to the LORD,
to the Creator of Heaven and earth,
praising Him for all His glory,
a glory He shares with all the earth
and all the creatures thereon.

The birds sing in joy
in the presence of the LORD,
in the light He brings to their eyes.
And the beasts of the field
rejoice, too, at His coming.

Why should they not rejoice
that their Maker has come
to dwell with man
and with all His Creation?
What can they do but sing His praise?

This is as it should be,
as it was meant to be
from the time the LORD
uttered His first Word,
from the time He commanded light to shine forth.

And so we find our way
back to the Garden;
in this way the universe
finds its fulfillment –
all partake of the Tree of Life in joy.

The angels stand at our side
to bless us and to guide
our feet into the Kingdom of Heaven;
and they too rejoice as one
to see the fulfillment of Creation.

And the LORD rejoices over His creatures,
singing as one sings at festivals
for the glory come upon all Creation,
for the order of the universe
shining forth in His NAME.

How wonderful it is
when all live as one
in the One who made them!
It leaves us without words
to describe…

Hippie Convert (III)

It is perfect,
this we can say
in all truth;
it is filled with grace
and the light of His face.

Can you imagine
looking into the face of the LORD?
Can you imagine seeing Him before you?
You will see Him face to face
in all that surrounds you!

It has been said
that to look into the face of the poor
is to look into the face of God.
And this is true.
But the face of God is seen best in our enemy.

When I say "our enemy,"
I mean him who seems most against us.
(I think of how looking into the face of Esau,
who had pursued his life so tenaciously,
Jacob saw the face of God.)

For God is in all and everything.
Though quite apart from all things,
His glory shines in everything and everyone
and His face may be perceived everywhere
by the enlightened heart.

And our hearts will be enlightened
on that day the LORD comes,
on that day He fulfills
the oneness of all Creation –
we will not be able to look away.

This we should fear
if we still cling to this earth
and our own concept
of the oneness of all…
for that will be taken from us.

No more will false light shine;
no more will man be able to deny
the truth of God's presence
in the world
and in himself.

Epilogue

Come home, sweet hippie,
the LORD is calling you
away from the license you hold to so tightly
and into His loving arms,
where freedom is found.

Why should you be so faithful
to a love that is so false,
to an illusion that leaves you wanting
something of substance in your life?
Let the LORD take you to wife!

He is the world's only lover
worth the time of day –
all else will but lead you astray
into a yawning darkness
when its essence is revealed.

In Him you will find flowers
that do not wilt and fade,
that do not rot with the passage of time
but grow more beautiful
with each coming year.

Two Books

You have no reason to fear
the reach of His arms,
the light that surrounds you
in His glorious presence.
Here there is only hope and joy.

Put down the pipe
and take up the Cup;
you will only find truth and goodness
in His holy Blood.
There is no high like the heights of Heaven.

Let your heart be purified
by the touch of Christ:
Jesus is God,
He is the Resurrection and the Life,
and that life is upon us now.

You need look no further
than His wounds
to find the surpassing love
upon which you set your heart –
absolute peace is in His arms.

Other Books by James Kurt

Our Daily Bread:
Exposition of the Readings of Catholic Mass –
A page of writing for every Mass of the liturgical calendar for the Roman Rite; reflections drawn from the readings. 727 pp. 2004. w/ imprimatur.
Our Daily Bread: Lent –   86 pp. 2019. w/ imprimatur.

Prayers to the Saints (Updated) –
A page of prayer to each saint on the General Roman Calendar for the U.S.A.
237 pp.   2019 (original 2007).   w/ imprimatur.

"TURN and Become like Children":
Refuting the Presumed Contradictions of the Jerusalem Bible
Old Testament Commentary –
A case study recounting the problems afflicting modern biblical scholarship as exemplified in the JB. 188 pp. 2019.

"Into Your Hands…":
Distillation of the Letters of Fr. Jean-Pierre de Caussade –
Reflections of the profound counsel of Fr. de Caussade to embrace the Cross and find the Lord's will (and joy) even in our greatest sufferings. 82 pp. 2019.

Remembrance of Things Present –
A mystical work seeking the presence of the LORD in the moment, where He dwells at all times. 100 pp. 2018. w/ imprimatur.

Lines of Grace: Meditations on Verses of Holy Scripture,
The Stations of the Cross, and The Most Holy Rosary –
A Catholic devotional especially for the encouragement of the practice of plenary indulgence. 195 pp. 2016.

Christian Vision of the Old Testament –
Synopsis and exhortation; faith-filled overview of all books of the Old Testament as prefiguration of Jesus, with a focus on the prophetic nature of God's Word.
273 pp. 2013/2019. w/ imprimatur.

Blessed Guilt (A Universal Conversion Story) –
On the life-giving repentance found in Jesus' blood; vaguely autobiographical but without particulars, thus making it a universal story.
119 pp. 2013. w/ imprimatur.

Chapters of the Gospels –
Exposition of the four gospels, chapter by chapter;
in the style of *Our Daily Bread*.
114 pp. 2009. w/ imprimatur.

The Most Holy Trinity and The Four Corners of the Universe –
A collection of writings on the Trinity and its reflection in Creation;
founded upon the Shema. 300 pp. 2008. w/ imprimatur.

YHWH: Order of the Divine NAME –
On the significance of the contemplative silence that is the NAME of God,
and its application to a spiritual life. 260 pp. 2008/2019. w/ imprimatur.

Turn of the Jubilee Year: A Conversion Song –
Autobiographical depiction of vocation search through pilgrimage to Medjugorje
and stays at a hermitage or two. 230 pp. 2004.

Songs for Children of Light: *Ten Albums of Lyrics* –
White on black conceptual work with simple line drawings for each song.
150 pp. 2003.

silence in the city –
Short contemplative poems; moments of divine silence in the midst of city life.
148 pp. (74 pieces). 2003.

author's website:
www.writingsofjameskurt.org

podcasting site:
www.hermitinthecity.libsyn.com

blog site:
www.hippieconvert.wordpress.com

www.ingramcontent.com/pod-product-compliance
Lightning Source LLC
Chambersburg PA
CBHW030315080526
44584CB00012B/574